ANCIENT
ALIENS.

ANCIENT ALIENS®

THE OFFICIAL COMPANION BOOK

FROM
THE PRODUCERS OF
ANCIENT ALIENS®

HARPER**ELIXIR**
An Imprint of HarperCollinsPublishers

HARPER**ELIXIR**

HarperCollins books may be purchased for educational, business, or sales promotional use. For information, please e-mail the Special Markets Department at SPsales@harpercollins.com.

FIRST EDITION

Designed by Suet Yee Chong

Library of Congress Cataloging-in-Publication Data is available upon request.

ISBN 978–0–06–245541–3

16 17 18 19 20   RRD   10 9 8 7 6 5 4 3 2 1

CONTENTS

BURNS

n to tell me you have never heard of

producer, Nikki Boella, and her
tion on a documentary special for
nes and the Ultimate Quest. It was
to their first *Indiana Jones* film in
and the Kingdom of the Crystal Skull.
ent, would be producing it, and we
ust a making-of movie special.
ssic Pictures documentary? The one
h all of those rhetorical questions?"

stares and blank expressions. A
d. I had to accept the fact that my
he age of forty—and not one of
ken and his groundbreaking book

Now, I admit that—even by this time—I had not read the book. I had only seen the documentary back when I was in high school. Nevertheless, it made a huge impact on me.

For the Indiana Jones project, the folks at Lucasfilm wanted us to do a two-hour special, but they did not want to share with us any details about their upcoming film. Everything about their project was top secret. All they would share with us was the trailer and the movie poster. That was it.

"What could this new movie be

the door into another exciting area: ancient astronaut theory.

Believing that *Indiana Jones and the Kingdom of the Crystal Skull* would be borrowing much from Erich von Däniken, I asked Nikki to find us "the new Erich von Däniken." There must be someone, I reasoned, who is carrying his mantle into the twenty-first century.

Enter Giorgio Tsoukalos, a young man with a deep tan, an eager grin, and a mane of thick, restless hair.

After he gave his interview for our documentary, I asked to meet with him. "You really believe in all this aliens stuff?" I asked. "I do not believe," he said to me, using a combination of precise diction flavored with a vaguely traceable Euro-Swiss accent, "I know."

The documentary special premiered on May 18, 2008. It was well received, and everyone associated with it was proud to have been part of it.

Several weeks later, I had an opportunity to have lunch with an executive from History. It was then I confided that my inspiration for the Indiana Jones special was Erich von Däniken and *Chariots of the Gods*.

"I love *Chariots of the Gods*!" my client enthused. "I'd love to do a new *Chariots of the Gods* for television!"

Armed with this bit of good news, I dashed back to my office and called Giorgio.

"Is Erich von Däniken still alive?" I asked, gingerly.

"Absolutely!" replied the hirsute pop-icon-to-be. "He lives in Switzerland and I will be happy to arrange a phone call for you."

The rest, as they say, is History (Channel).

My phone conversation with Erich convinced me that a new approach to *Chariots of the Gods* was not only long overdue, it was imperative that it be done. Much work and research had been done in the field of ancient astronaut theory in the forty years since Erich's book had first been published, and since that time, humankind had landed on the moon—and even sent robots to Mars!

We would call our documentary *Ancient Aliens*. We also made a deliberate decision to not populate the program with the usual phalanx of naysayers, skeptics, and debunkers. Not because we didn't want balance, mind you. It was simply because we wanted our show to be open-minded.

For us, *Ancient Aliens* was—and remains—a show about questions and possibilities. It is about a theory. The big "What if?"

We knew from the start that we couldn't prove ancient astronaut theory any more than we could prove the resurrection of Jesus. It was an interpretation based on evidence.

The show premiered on March 8, 2009, and quickly became a hit.

One two-hour documentary special led to five more—and each of those was based on five rhetorical questions: Who were they? ("The Visitors.") Why did they come? ("The Mission.") What did they leave behind? ("The Evidence.") Where did they go? ("Closer Encounters.") Will they return? ("The Return.")

At this point, I thought we were finished. Six two-hour television documentaries about ancient astronaut theory. Even Sun Classic Pictures didn't accomplish that!

My client at History called again. "We need another ten hours."

After that there was another ten. And another. And another.

As of this writing, we are well past one hundred programs, and there is no end in sight.

"Ancient Aliens was— and remains—a show about questions and possibilities. It is about a theory. The big "What if?"

Have I become a believer? Let's just say I remain open-minded, just as I hope our audiences are. I think of myself as the narrator of the show. I deal only in facts—but I'm open to asking questions: Could it be? What if? How can we be sure? In this way our series remains honest. We let the ancient astronaut theorists have their day in court. We let them give answers to the questions we pose. Sometimes the answers are plausible. Sometimes they're outrageous. All of them are honestly held and thoughtfully given.

Shortly after the series premiered, I came across an article written by a history professor. In it, he accused our series of offering "pseudo science" and "pseudo history" and of having, what he termed, a "post-colonial" attitude. That is to say, he objected to our questioning of conventional history and suggesting that third-world peoples in ancient times could not have produced architectural wonders without the help of some kind of "superior, outside guidance."

Excuse me?

I think it's fair to remind those skeptics in our audience that it is not we, the producers of *Ancient Aliens*, who suggest that some sort of extraterrestrial intelligence inspired the building of ancient pyramids, tombs, and temples; it is the ancient astronaut theorists in the program who suggest that. And where do they get this notion from? Why, from the very walls of the pyramids, tombs, and temples!

We don't say extraterrestrials created humankind. Ancient texts and scriptures say that.

In fact, ancient astronaut theory is no more audacious than the theologies of just about every religion in the world, and both are ultimately as connected to science and archaeology as they are to each other. All of them are looking for proof of humankind's origins. All of them are looking for God.

As the series creator and executive producer of *Ancient Aliens*, I am frequently asked if I believe in the stories we tell—if I believe in ancient astronaut theory.

My answer is simple: I'm open to it.

According to the Greek philosopher Plato, his mentor, Socrates, believed that "a man knew everything who admitted he knew nothing." I believe there is much about our history—and our origins—that we still don't know. But one fact is certain: our world is filled with architectural riddles and scientific anomalies. Science and religion each attempt to provide answers to the profound questions of the universe. *Ancient Aliens* attempts to answer these same questions but with a unique and profound filter: What if intelligent beings had existed on this planet thousands of years ago? What if they influenced our past and guided our future?

As we ask at the beginning of each new episode of our series . . .

What if it were true?

All we ask is that you, our audience, keep an open mind.

INTRODUCTION

Millions of people around the world believe we have been visited in the past by extraterrestrial beings. What if it were true? Did ancient aliens really help to shape our history? And if so, what if there were clues left behind . . . sometimes hiding in plain sight? What if we could find the evidence?

Each week, hundreds of thousands of viewers tune in to History's wildly popular hit show *Ancient Aliens*, seeking insight into those very questions—and to become part of a compelling, probative conversation about the mysteries that surround us.

Throughout recorded history, archaeologists have discovered fascinating and bizarre structures—as well as carvings and texts—that have forced us to question the established notions of the past. Ruins dating back thousands of years reveal engineering skill that surpasses even our most modern technological capabilities. Religious texts from diverse, ancient cultures tell incredibly similar stories of gods descending from the heavens in fiery crafts. Ancient rock art depicts figures that resemble modern-day astronauts. And mysterious monoliths—many placed in alignment with heavenly constellations—dot the landscapes of nearly every continent.

In his 1968 book, *Chariots of the Gods*, Swiss author Erich von Däniken proposed that all of this evidence pointed to one profound but logical possibility: extraterrestrials visited Earth in the distant past and so changed the course of human history. This concept—later known as ancient astronaut theory—is today embraced by literally millions of people around the world.

Ancient Aliens®: The Official Companion Book has been carefully researched and edited by the producers of *Ancient Aliens* in an effort to give both hard-core fans and open-minded enthusiasts as complete—and equally satisfying—an experience as the one they receive while watching a one-hour weekly episode. We have gone into our own "ancient" archives and pulled a number of the interviews we conducted with our top contributors during the course of our eight-year run.

Because much of the material discussed during these interviews had to be trimmed down to conform to the limitations of a forty-three-minute television episode, we are now able to give readers the benefit of a more in-depth discussion—one that digs even deeper into topics ranging from Neolithic monoliths to stargates, from Egyptian pyramids to UFOs.

The stories in this book are told directly, as they were told to us, by the very best proponents of ancient astronaut theory. They represent thousands of hours of research—as well as centuries of human knowledge.

While reading them you may once again find yourself asking:

Who were they?
Why did they come?
What did they leave behind?
Where did they go?
Will they return?

ERICH VON DÄNIKEN

EZEKIEL'S WHEEL

In 1968, just one year before Neil Armstrong's epic moon walk, a book was published that forever changed the way many in the scientific, religious, and creative communities would view their home planet. Written by Swiss author Erich von Däniken, *Chariots of the Gods* attempted to prove that alien explorers had visited Earth thousands of years ago. This theory caused a sensation and launched a prolific career that includes forty books, which have sold more than 65 million copies around the world.

Von Däniken's tireless curiosity and controversial theories about the unexplained mysteries of our ancient cultures have captured the attention of the world—and ignited a movement known as ancient astronaut theory.

Many years ago, I gave a speech at NASA, in Huntsville, Alabama. During this speech, I spoke briefly about Ezekiel, the biblical prophet and author of the book of Ezekiel. I touched on Ezekiel's famed vision of a fiery chariot descending from the heavens—and how we can now see that this is a description of advanced technology for which Ezekiel himself did not possess the language.

Later, at dinner, Joe Blumrich, one of NASA's chief engineers at the time, said to me, "Erich, that was very interesting. I had never heard the story of Ezekiel. But in the Bible you will definitely not find any examples of technology. You see, the Bible—those are visions. Those are dreams. Those are stories, not reality." But still, he said, "Next time I go on vacation, I'll read the book of Ezekiel." Later he told me, "The first two or three pages, I was just laughing." But then he got to the passage where Ezekiel describes the wheels of the Splendor of the Highest.

In the book of Ezekiel, you see, Ezekiel writes that he saw a fiery chariot, or vehicle, come out of the clouds. He calls this vehicle the Splendor of the Highest. In the original text, in Hebrew, he never uses the word "God." He always speaks about "the highest" or "the one." The word "God" is used in German or English translations, where the vehicle is called the Splendor of God, but not in the Hebrew original. When the Splendor of the Highest descends, it creates a noise that Ezekiel compares to the thundering of a waterfall. On top of the Splendor of the Highest, he sees something like a capsule. He describes it as looking like a diamond. Inside the glittering diamond he sees something like a throne. And on the throne, he sees a figure sitting *like a human*, wearing glittering clothes. Ezekiel always uses the word "like," because he does not have the words to describe directly what he sees. Then he describes the vehicle—the Splendor of the Highest.

The Splendor of the Highest had four wheels. These wheels were what caught Joe Blumrich's attention. Ezekiel describes the wheels and says it looked as if one wheel were in the middle of another wheel. And they turned to every side, without turning the wheel itself. Without making a steering movement. So the wheel went forward, backward, left, and right, but never made a steering movement. Ezekiel was really fascinated by the wheels; he describes the wheels four times. This interested Blumrich, who was thinking a lot about the challenges of wheels on space vehicles.

When you travel from Earth to Mars,

Ezekiel's vision of the Splendor of the Highest is the inaugural vision in the Book of Ezekiel. In this engraving of the vision, a representation of the four wheels can be seen in the upper right corner.

for example, you don't know exactly where you'll land, not down to the meter. Maybe you land in rocks. And you cannot move around in a curve. You want to break out of your ring of rock, but you are surrounded. You cannot move in a curve, so you need a wheel that can navigate exactly on the centimeter like this. And that's exactly what Ezekiel describes. Inspired by Ezekiel, Blumrich would later go on to design and patent a similar wheel, called the Omni Wheel.

We can now see this is a description of advanced technology.

Ezekiel describes the Splendor of the Highest from chapter 1 to chapter 39. After its first visitation, the Splendor of the Highest returns a second time. Ezekiel writes that on the second visit, the hands of the highest took him away. So in my opinion, now he's sitting in the Splendor of the Highest, next to the pilot. Then they lift off. Ezekiel feels the pressure on his chest. He says, "And the hands of the highest were pressing onto my chest." They fly to a very, very high mountain. Up there, he sees beneath him something like a little city. And in the center of the city is something like a temple. They fly over this little city, come to a standstill over the temple, and slowly descend. And on that occasion, Ezekiel recounts that the noise of the wings was doubly as loud as it had been in the desert. After a few minutes they again come to a standstill.

When he exits the Splendor of the Highest, there is another one of the humanlike beings in glittering clothes. The being greets Ezekiel by laughing. He says, "Ah, human. You have eyes to see, but you see nothing. You have ears to hear, but you hear nothing." And the being has a strange measuring instrument in his hands. In Bible translations now, you can read that it was a measuring instrument, like a cord. It's probably not a cord, but it's something with which you can measure, and the stranger, in the glittering clothes, commands Ezekiel, the human, to measure the whole building on which they landed—the whole temple.

Ezekiel in the meantime now knows that this being is not God. So he's not afraid. He has courage, and he asks him: Why? Why should I measure this building? And the stranger says that that's why we brought you here, human; to do this job. So Ezekiel measures the building, and the beings return him to his people.

In chapter 40 of the book of Ezekiel, you find every measurement of the building: length, width, stairs, floors—it's incredible. There are just pages and pages of measurements. A German engineer, Hans Herbert Beier, who, along with a group of other engineers, constructs large buildings in Germany, read Ezekiel's measurements of the temple and wondered if he could actually build an architecturally sound building based on those measurements. He wondered,

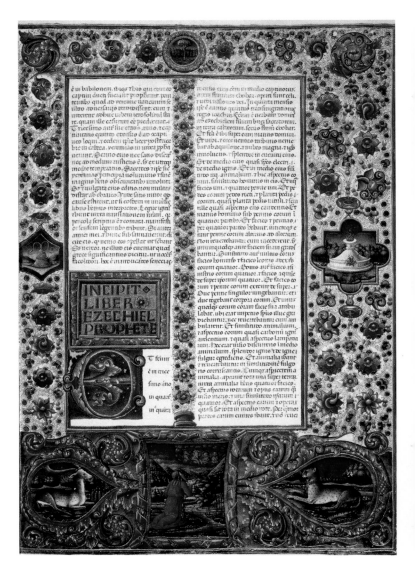

A fifteenth-century illuminated manuscript of the Book of Ezekiel, illuminated by Taddeo Crivelli (1425–1479) and others, depicting Ezekiel's vision bottom center. Across the centuries, artists and religious scribes have continued to depict Ezekiel's visions.

"Is this something we could use or was it just the product of imagination?" He started to reconstruct Ezekiel's temple inch by inch to scale, until they had a complete model of it. It was absolutely incredible. It's absolutely amazing—we know today what Ezekiel really saw. It was not a vision. He did not imagine it.

At the time of his experience with the Splendor of the Highest, Ezekiel—along with much of the rest of the Jews—was a captive of Babylonia. He worked as a slave, in exile from Jerusalem and his home. His people were very downtrodden. After the extraterrestrials brought Ezekiel back to his people, they believed he had come into contact with the almighty God, because they did not understand a word of technology. Upon his return they asked him, "What has been done to you? Have you suffered? Were you hungry? Were you thirsty?" And Ezekiel says, "No. I was brought to a very, very high mountain. I had to take the measurements of a building. Here are the results." Because his community believed that Ezekiel was conveying the word of God, that text never went into the trash. It entered the holy literature of humankind.

We know today what Ezekiel really saw. It was not a vision. He did not imagine it.

And that's exactly what they wanted, the extraterrestrials. They knew that thousands of years in the future the followers of Ezekiel would have their own technology. They would be able to fly, they would have satellites around their planet, and so forth. And in that future, the people would re-read their old texts, their holy texts, and say, *Come on. This is not God. We are believers, but not believers in stupidity. God is much bigger. God is not explainable.* This writing has to do with technology. They are talking about wings, about noise, about metal elements, and so on: this is technology.

According to the old traditions, a few humans were undoubtedly abducted by extraterrestrials. They were taken from the Earth, up to another place. Of course, these humans never used the word "spaceship"

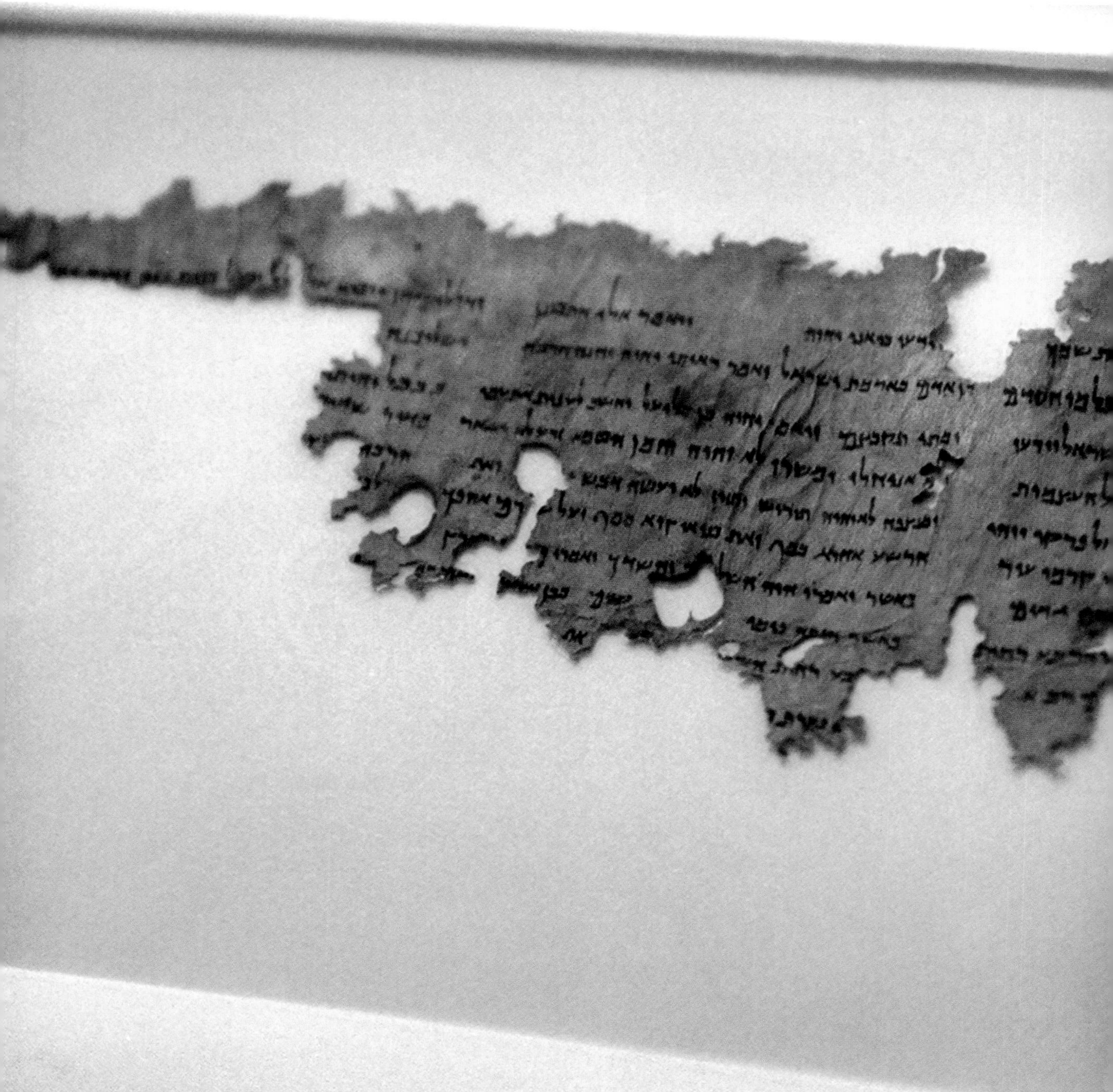

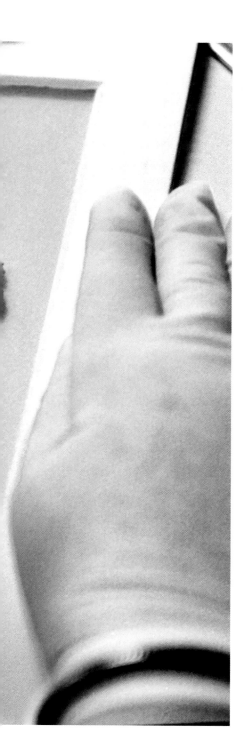

because they had no word like "spaceship," but they explained what happened. One case is Abraham—he was taken up. Another case is Ezekiel. The question is, Why? Why were these gentlemen thousands of years ago being abducted? Because what they saw had to enter into the holy religion.

Only the holy religion—the books, the texts of the holy religion—would survive thousands and thousands of years. In the past, the E.T.s left what I would call a time capsule, maybe at one or more places. How could you be sure that this time capsule would be found by a generation in the far future? The generation of the future first has to *know* that there is a time capsule from the past. If you don't know anything, you will never seek. That's why, in the holy text, it has to be written down: *I was abducted. They brought me there and there. I had to measure this building. Here is the measuring data.* The future generation—us—should ask the question: Is it possible we have been visited by beings from outer space?

An Israeli conservation worker prepares a scrap of one of the Dead Sea Scrolls, recounting the prophet Ezekiel in conversation with God, for exhibition at the Rockefeller Museum in Jerusalem in 1997. The Dead Sea Scrolls, which date back to between the third century BC and first century AD, were discovered between 1947 and 1956 in eleven caves along the Dead Sea in Israel. They are the oldest group of Old Testament manuscripts ever found.

GIORGIO A. TSOUKALOS

THE EGYPTIAN CONNECTION

Giorgio A. Tsoukalos became fascinated with archaeology and ancient history at a young age, while traveling the world with his family from their home in Switzerland. As a teenager, Tsoukalos read about ancient astronaut theory and began attending lectures and conferences by Erich von Däniken. Working together, Tsoukalos and von Däniken cofounded a research society in 1998, and Tsoukalos served as a representative for the Swiss author in the English-speaking world.

Tsoukalos is the publisher of *Legendary Times Magazine*, the world's only ancient astronaut research journal. His passion for research and exploration has taken him to over sixty countries in search of evidence of extraterrestrial contact in our distant past.

THE PYRAMIDS

According to scholars, the Great Pyramid of Khufu in Giza, Egypt, was built on what is considered to be the center of all the landmasses of Earth. The massive structure is almost perfectly aligned to true north. Inside the pyramid, the designers added small shafts aligned toward two specific constellations, Orion and Sirius.

Mainstream Egyptologists believe it took only twenty-two years to build the Great Pyramid. If that were the case, the Egyptians would have had to cut, transport, and put into place one stone block every ninety seconds. And that is providing no holidays, no rest, no nothing—just twenty-four hours a day for twenty-two years. And anyone who knows anything about construction processes would say that isn't really possible.

Another interesting fact is that inside the Grand Gallery of the Giza pyramid, we find the most massive of stones—I mean, huge pieces of rock that were placed next to one another. Now, rock has a natural grain inside of it. So let's say you cut a rock at the quarry, and you cut it through the natural grain and one line goes horizontally. What is fascinating is that inside the Grand Gallery, you can find two pieces of rock next to each other where the grain goes from one rock to the next without any loss of material. How is that done? If you have a thick, thick blade or a chisel and a hammer—crude tools—you would be unable to achieve that result. And there are multiple spots inside the Grand Gallery where this grain is continuous; there is no loss of material. That is sensational, but nobody talks about it.

Now, what do the ancient texts tell us about who or for what purpose

A satellite view of the Giza pyramid complex outside of Cairo, Egypt. According to scholars, the Great Pyramid of Khufu was built on the center of all the landmasses of Earth—and the three pyramids align perfectly with the stars of Orion's Belt in the Orion constellation.

these pyramids were built? We have one very detailed description of how these massive stones were transported from the quarry to the building site, and it reads that the master builders had the capability of putting some type of a white, powderlike substance onto the stones, and some "magical incantations" were spoken. And then they basically gave the stone block a push and it moved by six feet as if by magic. Now, again, did it really move by magic? No, something happened there. Some technology was implemented. What was it exactly? I haven't a clue.

There is absolutely no question that the Great Pyramids of Giza were built by human beings. The ancient Egyptians did it. However, what the ancient Egyptian texts also tell us is that the Egyptians did it with the assistance of "the Guardians of the Sky," as the texts refer to them. Those extraterrestrials descended from the skies to help the Egyptians with the technology and the planning of those monuments, because, we have to understand, the technological frame of reference of our ancestors was infinitely smaller than the technological frame of reference we have today.

Mainstream Egyptologists believe it took only twenty-two years to build the Great Pyramid. If that were the case, the Egyptians would have had to cut, transport, and put into place one stone block every ninety seconds.

With everything in our history, there is a clear evolution in technology. Meaning, you start out simple and then you end up with something really sophisticated. I always liken it to the Ford Model T and the Ford Taurus. The Model T was the first affordable, mass-produced car. Today in the Ford family we have the Taurus. If you compare the Model T to any modern car of the twenty-first century, the two of them are in different galaxies. But we have a clear evolution of technology.

We started out rather simplistic, and now here we are today with modern cars that are technically complex, fuel-efficient, and so on. But if you go back five thousand years, that evolution of technology is reversed.

At first you have monolithic gigantic blocks, some of them weighing five hundred–plus tons, requiring extraordinary engineering capabilities. But then later, people started to use brick-size blocks, resorting to simpler technology. Why? What happened there? That is not an ordinary evolution in technology.

Almost out of nowhere, our ancestors were building pyramids with the most gigantic stone blocks. Stone blocks that we today would have great difficulty replicating. I'm not suggesting that today we cannot do this, because of course we can. But we would use the most sophisticated, most advanced computer technology and machinery in order to accomplish it. When our ancestors tell us that they had help from elsewhere, we should listen to that. Because they're very clear in stating that they received help from above. And by "above," I don't mean some type of spiritual or divine beings—not at all. Our ancestors erroneously *thought* they were being visited by divine beings or by "gods." In reality, they misinterpreted being visited by advanced space travelers.

What we're being told by modern-day archaeology or by modern-day Egyptology is different from what the ancient historians wrote down. For example, the Greek historian Herodotus said that the pyramids were built by the ancient Egyptians but with the assistance of the Guardians of the Sky. In fact, according to Herodotus, the Egyptians credited a king named Saurid rather than the pharaoh Cheops. And Saurid is the one who built the pyramids alongside the Guardians of the Sky. He was the master builder and he instructed his people on all the details of how to build pyramids. But according to some ancient Egyptian historians, he received all this knowledge from the Guardians of the Sky, and, according to ancient astronaut theory, these guardians were nothing else but space travelers.

One very interesting aspect about this whole Saurid story is that the Egyptians are very clear in stating that Saurid is the same person that the Hebrews called Enoch. So we have a correlation between two cultures, and they all speak of the same thing. If you read the book of Enoch and

SKYSCRAPERS OF THE ANCIENTS

Far out on the Giza Plateau, in the desert on the outskirts of what is modern-day Cairo, Egypt, loom three of the most familiar and yet most mysterious megalithic structures in the world: the great pyramids of Egypt, like three bronze mountains orphaned on the plain. The Great Pyramid of Khufu, the oldest and largest of the three, towers four hundred and eighty feet above the sand, or as high as a fifty-story skyscraper. Weighing in at six and a half million tons, it took two and a half million blocks of stone to build the structure. And those two and a half million blocks of stone? They are believed to have come from a quarry five hundred miles away from the site of the pyramids. The average weight of each stone is an astonishing two and a half tons, with the heaviest stone weighing in at an estimated fifty to eighty tons.

The Great Pyramid is one of the greatest marvels of architectural engineering in world history. And yet archaeologists have long speculated about how the ancient Egyptians were able to build such a structure. In today's largest construction sites and quarries, massive mega-machines are used to dig, cut, and lift stone. These man-made vehicles dwarf their builders and perform the work of thousands of men, using modern hydraulic technology. Without equipment such as bulldozers, cranes, forklifts, and excavators, builders could never construct modern skyscrapers.

According to Egyptologists, the civilization that built the pyramids, however, had not yet invented the wheel, did not have pulleys, and had not discovered iron. Mainstream Egyptologists believe that ancient Egyptians built the pyramids with only the simplest of tools: stone balls, copper chisels, rope. But with these limited tools, how did they cut enormous blocks of stone with such precision? How did they transport enormous blocks of stone hundreds of miles on sand and then lift them precisely into place?

In fact, there is little consensus among mainstream historians and Egyptologists as to the actual tools and methods used in constructing the pyramids. Despite years of research and study, archaeologists and Egyptologists remain uncertain.

you read what is written about Saurid, the stories coincide. This is not a coincidence. Both stories relate that they had contact with flesh-and-blood extraterrestrials. They saw something and then they relayed it in their books, each using the words that they had at their disposal at the time.

Our ancestors, number one, had a completely different technological frame of reference from us. And number two, they didn't have the words for things like cranes. At the time, they didn't have the words for engines or machines or motors or helicopter blades or fuel pumps. So they described whatever they saw with the vocabulary they had access to that best described whatever it was they were witnessing. And this is why we have such bizarre stories today of things flying up in the sky, or things descending, or people falling to the ground because the Earth was trembling and there was a lot of noise, fire, and whirling dust and wind. People thought they had a divine encounter, when in reality it was no such thing.

One question we must ask ourselves is how the inside of the pyramid was lit, because the deeper you go inside, the darker it gets, and after only a few corners, after walking through these shafts, it gets pitch-dark. There is no light in there from the outside. Suggestions have been made that the ancient Egyptians used copper mirrors in every corner of the corridors, diverting the sunlight from the outside all the way inside. However, the copper mirrors that were found from ancient Egyptian times were very dull. They weren't highly polished mirrors as we are familiar with today. There have been researchers who have actually set up these real-life experiments where they determined pretty quickly that if these mirrors were indeed placed in these shafts, after only three or four corners, the sunlight would have dissipated and disappeared. So that theory didn't hold up.

The Dendera Light, depicted on a stone relief located deep within the Hathor temple in Dendera, Egypt. Because of its striking resemblance to a modern-day lightbulb, some scholars believe this relic is proof of ancient Egyptian electrical technology that could have been used to navigate through the dark corridors of the pyramids.

The second theory was that they just used torches, but that would mean you would find remnants of soot on the ceilings. As we understand it, though, no remnants of soot have ever been found. Even when they tested for microscopic remnants, they didn't find anything. So the only remaining conclusion is that the ancient Egyptians lit the inside with some type of an artificial light source. Why am I discussing this? Is there evidence for an artificial light source? The answer is yes.

In Dendera, Egypt, there's an underground crypt that depicts what looks like a modern-day lightbulb. It shows a bulbous object with a snake inside and a stalk or a cable that goes underneath to a type of box. People have suggested that this stalk is a cable going to some type of an electrical device, a battery, and that this whole object is a depiction of a modern-day lightbulb. The Austrian engineer Walter Garn actually was able to re-create this bulb with the resources available to the ancient Egyptians—quite fascinating. What's even more fascinating is that the hieroglyphics surrounding these carvings all say that this is the bringer of light. And by the way, that crypt in which they found those carvings is underground and it was always called the Secret Chamber of Secret Knowledge. Only the high priests had access to those panels. Why? Is it because the high priests were the initiates who had direct contact with extraterrestrials who were taught how to handle these types of technology?

My colleague, Chris Dunn, has suggested that the whole Giza Plateau is some sort of power plant. Others have suggested that the reason we have pyramids and obelisks all around the world is that they have acted as some type of wireless technology stations—relay stations that would transmit the power from one place to another. And this is partly due to their crystalline properties. Now, do I personally think that that was the case? I don't know. I'm more of a nuts-and-bolts basic kind of guy, as in, sure, these might've been used for some type of power relay stations, and that's highly fascinating, but the main question I have is, How was it done? Because these things originate from a time when, according to mainstream archaeologists, we were carving with chicken bones. I'm being facetious with the chicken bones, but even a copper tool doesn't work on a granite boulder, you know, if it requires cutting. So the copper tool, in my opinion, is akin to a chicken

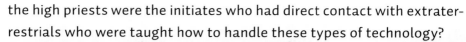

A view of all six pyramids of the Giza pyramid complex on the outskirts of Cairo, Egypt. In front, the smaller "three Queens" pyramids, and behind, from left to right, the Pyramid of Menkaure, the Pyramid of Khafre, and the Great Pyramid of Khufu.

The Pyramid of the Sun at the Teotihuacan complex in Mexico. A stepped pyramid, the Temple of the Sun is the third largest pyramid in the world. Over two thousand years old, much about its purpose and function remain a mystery, including why it was built over a man-made tunnel that leads to a chamber almost twenty feet beneath the center of the pyramid.

bone. It's physically impossible that it worked. We are talking about physics. You cannot cut a dense stone with a material that is softer than the stone in question.

The shape of a pyramid is one of the most telling common threads that we have in the entire ancient astronaut theory, because pyramids exist worldwide. They exist not only where cultures were flourishing, but also in places where at times there were no cultures flourishing and all of a sudden you find pyramid shapes. For example, in Central America they have stepped pyramids, and the ancient ziggurats of Sumer were also stepped. We have pyramids in China and in ancient Greece. Ecuador is filled with pyramids inside the jungle that to this day have remained unexplored. The Cholula Pyramid in Mexico is the world's largest monument ever constructed by human hands. In fact, the volume of the Cholula Pyramid—the whole pyramid complex—is 4.45 million cubic meters. The great pyramid in Egypt has only 2.5 million cubic meters in volume.

The question is, Why? How is it that all around the world we find these similar structures? Because it doesn't matter where we go, the construction styles are almost identical. It's as if all these ancient builders went to the same school.

Or, as the ancient astronaut theory suggests, these people were all visited by the same teachers—the same extraterrestrials—and

given these design ideas in order to build monuments that would withstand time. Because in my opinion all of these pyramids are nothing but calling cards for the future. They're incredible feats of technology and engineering, and a society with no evolution in technology would not really be able to pull them off without an evolution in technology. So the question then becomes, Is it possible that the knowledge to build these structures was given by beings from above? And by that, I'm 100 percent referring to flesh-and-blood extraterrestrials.

Another very intriguing fact is that many of the ancient pyramids either align or are built in some reference to the Orion and Sirius constellations. Why? The answer to that might be that those extraterrestrials came from those constellations. So there is a strong possibility that extraterrestrials did come from exactly those spots in our galaxy.

Were the areas around these pyramids landing sites? Is that why the Chinese and Egyptians both oriented their pyramids toward Orion and Sirius? There may have been a connection. To me, this is evidence that flesh-and-blood extraterrestrials traveled around the Earth, sharing this knowledge with different ancient cultures.

When there are pyramids all around the world, to attribute that simply to coincidence is a cop-out. It is incredible to suggest that all of a sudden they all just woke up and decided to create these shapes in the form of pyramids. So the fact that they all look similar and have these bizarre stories in conjunction with those pyramid shapes, I think that we have to start looking at these symbols and ask, How did they originate and from where?

THE SPHINX

The Sphinx has enchanted humankind for centuries. One of the things I find fascinating about the Sphinx is that when you read some of the earliest historians' works, while they report about the pyramids, they mysteriously leave out the Sphinx. Could this mean that in the era of the ancient Egyptians there were periods when the Sphinx was covered with sand and nobody knew of its existence? If you think about that for a moment, it's highly fascinating, because what did that thing look like at the time it was built or right after it was built? Some scholars have also suggested that the current head on the Sphinx's body is way too small for it to be proportional to the massive body. So all these theories have been proposed that maybe at first, instead of it being a human head, it was the head of a lion, or some other being. Who knows what else has happened over the long, long history of the Sphinx?

The Sphinx shows signs of water erosion created by rain, which is evidence that it must predate 2500 BC.

What was the Sphinx for? Why was it built? It's an incredible monument. It's fantastic. It's intricate. There *is* a story behind it—but what is the story? And personally, I'm not sure what the answer is.

What I am sure about is archaeologist Robert Schoch's theory that the Sphinx by far predates 2500 BC, the approximate date mainstream archaeologists believe that it was built. Schoch believes that the Sphinx shows signs of water erosion, which he believes was created by rain, which is evidence that it must predate 2500 BC.

If we are to subscribe to the idea that the Sphinx displays markings of water erosion, then that means that what's staring us in the face is much, much older than what mainstream science proposes. That alone is sensa-

tional because it means that our entire race goes back much further in time than what we've been told—and that our society goes back much further in time too.

Some have also proposed that there is a mirror image of the Giza Plateau on Mars, with the three pyramids and even what may appear to be a Sphinx. Now, if that were true, then that would have tremendous implications for us as a human race. I'm on the fence, but if the story of three pyramids and what appears to be a Sphinx on Mars is true, then that will be the perfect calling card for someone to make the extraterrestrial connection.

DAVID HATCHER CHILDRESS

THE MYSTERIES OF PERU

Author, publisher, and explorer, David Hatcher Childress has traveled the world several times over looking for adventure— and for answers to history's greatest mysteries. Born in France and raised in the United States, Childress has lived and worked all over the world including in Asia, Africa, the Middle East, and South America.

Childress's extensive research in Bolivia and Peru has made him a leading authority on signs of a possible ancient astronaut connection among the area's ancient ruins.

Over eight hundred remarkably straight lines are etched onto the surface of the Nazca Plain. Some of the straight lines extend as many as thirty miles. Two intersecting trapezoids intersect to form an X in the lower right corner, while multiple lines can be seen at bottom center and on the left-hand side of the image.

The Nazca Plain on the coast of southern Peru is really one of the greatest mysteries of South America. It goes for about fifty miles, and there are hundreds of geoglyphs and biomorphs—lines and figures—that are etched on the desert ground there. Some of them are simple straight lines; others are trapezoids, figures, and spirals. Some of the lines extend for hundreds of miles toward Tiahuanaco (also known as Tiwanaku) and Puma Punku. We can't be exactly sure who made the Nazca lines or when.

Mainstream archaeologists think that the Nazca lines were made by the Nazca people sometime between AD 400 and 650. Making the lines would certainly seem to be something that primitive people could do. All they would need to do, essentially, is expose a layer of soil that's just underneath the surface. By digging six to ten inches into the surface of the desert, they'd be able to expose a lighter soil, which would create these lines. Why would the Nazca people have done this? Well, mainstream archaeologists say that they were mapping out underground water, or that they were making ecological pleas to the sky gods for fertility or a good crop or good hunting. The area is very much a desert.

One of the strangest things about the Nazca lines is that they're seen well really only from the air. When you're actually at Nazca, it's a desert and kind of drab, and it's not like you're seeing something all that interesting. But once you get into an airplane,

A biomorph of a monkey at Nazca. At the time the geoglyphs and biomorphs were made, monkeys are not believed to have been present in the Nazca area—their habitat was hundreds of miles away in the Amazon rain forest.

you take off, and you're five hundred feet over the plain and looking down, the whole world changes. You're just seeing all of these lines and figures and trapezoids, and there are these giant figures, some of which—like the monkey—don't even exist there, but are native to the Amazon, thousands of miles away over the Andes. It's really exciting, and you're in a sense of wonder—like, *Wow, this is amazing.* And you really get excited seeing all this, and you're not sure exactly why. They're just a bunch of lines in the desert, but they seem to be of such a big scope and part of some grandiose plan that's there, but you can't figure out what it is. It's fascinating.

There *are* certain hills to the east of Nazca where you can climb up and see some of the nearby figures, but you really can't get a good idea of the scope of the area unless you're in an airplane. So when you're thinking of Nazca, you have to think, *Yes, whatever's going on here, it's some kind of signaling to the sky gods.* Adding to the mystery is that some of the Nazca lines extend for hundreds of miles, perfectly straight, as if they're following some energy line or ley line through the desert and over the mountains. They even go over cliff faces and rocky areas, obstacles you would think they would go around. But they go over areas where a person wouldn't be able to walk on the line itself. It's almost as if they were etched from an airship with a beam or something cutting a straight line into the desert. Here we may have some evidence that some high technology was used in creating the Nazca lines from above. So what is the purpose of all this?

The Sun-Star glyph at Nazca. Its composition of multiple overlapping geometric shapes bears an uncanny resemblance to a mandala or yantra.

A PELICAN AS LONG AS THREE FOOTBALL FIELDS

In 1927, the young Peruvian archaeologist Toribio Mejia Xesspe was hiking in the arid Nazca desert in southern Peru when he stumbled upon the Nazca lines—a discovery that would puzzle the archaeological world for decades. From his vantage point atop a plateau that stretched for nearly fifty bleak miles, he saw an immense network of clearly man-made ancient geoglyphs, or drawings etched into the earth. Though he was high above the valley floor, he was still not high enough to see the geoglyphs in their entirety and thus make out what the drawings were—but it was clear that an ancient people had labored with enormous skill to create the images and patterns of lines.

Years later, when airplane travel over the region became more frequent, the extent of his discovery was realized. Scattered over a nearly two-hundred-square-mile area was an expanse of eight hundred long, perfectly straight lines that stretched for miles, over valleys and mountains, accompanied by three hundred intricate, geometric patterns, and seventy animal and plant designs. The largest of the figures, a pelican, was almost the size of three football fields. The figures and patterns were of such oversize dimension that they could be recognized for what they were only from far above, in the sky.

The Nazca people who created these geoglyphs mysteriously disappeared around AD 500. When they did, their capital, Cahuachi, fell into disarray. Fourteen hundred

years later, anthropologists went to Cahuachi to study the ancient Nazca civilization, perhaps hoping to discover the reasons for their disappearance. Yet what they found has only deepened the mysteries of the Nazca: human skeletons with strangely elongated skulls, twice the size of a regular person's. From the enormous lines that cross the desert to the eerie skulls unearthed in its soil, the mysteries of Peru continue to challenge mainstream archaeology.

Well, one of the most interesting Nazca lines is the Sun-Star glyph. Because it's in a remote area, not many tourists who fly over the Nazca lines see it. But it is, by far, the strangest and most mathematically precise of all the glyphs at Nazca. It is very obviously a kind of mandala or yantra, symbols from ancient India or Tibet. And, in fact, yantras and mandalas are associated with coding and with flight, machinery, mechanisms, and devices. "Yantra" means "a device." In ancient India, yantras are associated with vimanas, the ancient airships that were written about in the Ramayana, the Mahabharata, and other ancient Indian texts. It's very interesting to think about what a mandala or yantra glyph is doing in the remote desert of Peru. In my mind, it would appear that there is a connection between the lines at Nazca and ancient India and the vimanas, that the Sun-Star is a code—a yantra—etched into the desert, that can be seen only from the sky.

Another figure that is particularly interesting is El Astronauta, or "The Spaceman"—a humanoid that appears to be wearing a big space helmet, who has one arm up as if he's waving. And it would seem that this is one of the sky gods. Or if he's not one of the sky gods himself, he's one of the Nazca people who is waving to the sky gods and saying, *Hi, we're here. Come and land. We know you came here before—come back. We want to see you again.*

So in many ways it would seem that Nazca is like a giant desert Etch A Sketch on which people have been making these gigantically huge figures to attract attention from the sky. And in a way they're signals. They're saying,

THE OWL-MAN

One hundred feet long, El Astronauta ("The Astronaut") is perched on a hill near the Nazca plateau and is visible from the Peruvian coast. Most mainstream archaeologists refer to the Nazca astronaut as "The Owl-Man," a name given to it by Maria Reiche in her book *The Mysteries of the Desert* (1949), which included the first aerial photograph of the biomorph.

This is where we are. It's very much like waving to somebody and saying, *Hey, I'm over here.* The mystery of the Nazca lines isn't really in their creation—drawing the lines wouldn't have been difficult to accomplish, unlike hauling giant megalithic blocks around—but instead, the mystery is in their purpose. A lot of effort went into creating the lines. I believe the purpose was to signal the gods, to signal the extraterrestrials in their airships and say, "Here we are. Land here."

There is a rather interesting theory about Nazca that explains it as a very early cargo cult. Cargo cults became more common during World War II in Melanesia, when these islands were at the geographical center of the struggle for control of the Pacific. Japanese, British, Australian, and American military forces came to these remote islands, built airstrips, and started landing cargo planes and bombers. They would get the natives to help them build these airstrips. And in exchange, they would give them T-shirts and other clothing items, cans of corned beef, and various things that the military had lying around. The natives were thrilled to get all this stuff. And then when the war ended, the military suddenly pulled out of these islands. All the planes and everyone left, and things went back to the very sleepy normal life that was on these little islands before the war. The natives then would go to the chief and say, *What was that all about?* These planes came here. The natives didn't really understand World War II—what all the fighting was about—but they liked the fact that these planes came out of the sky and brought them stuff. And they wanted the planes to return.

Nazca is like a giant desert Etch A Sketch.

In response, the chiefs on these islands created a kind of modern religion, which we now know as cargo cults. The chiefs said, *Well, that was our ancestors sending cargo from the gods out of the sky to us.* The chiefs then said, *To get these planes to come back out of the sky with all this good stuff they were bringing us, we need to attract these planes again.* What they would do was build models of airplanes out of bamboo

THE LADY OF THE LINES

In 1994, UNESCO declared the Nazca lines a World Heritage site, protecting these mysterious and awe-inspiring works for the benefit of the future and the shared legacy of humankind. But this may have never happened without the tireless efforts of Maria Reiche, a German researcher who was one of the first people to bring global attention to the Nazca lines—and to fight for their preservation. Reiche, who spoke five languages and studied mathematics, astronomy, and geography, began her work at Nazca as an assistant to the American scholar and historian Paul Kosok, the first serious researcher to study the Nazca lines.

After Kosok discontinued his work at Nazca in 1948, Maria Reiche continued her research and advocacy: she discovered eighteen new geoglyphs and persuaded the Peruvian Air Force to take aerial surveys and photographs of the lines, then wrote a book based on her research. With the proceeds from her book, Reiche campaigned to officially protect the geoglyphs, hiring guards out of her own pocket to patrol them. After the Peruvian government cut part of the Pan-American Highway through one of the geoglyphs, Reiche spent large sums of her own money to lobby and educate officials and the public about the lines and to further protect them from encroaching traffic. Having succeeded in convincing the government to restrict public access to the area, Reiche went on to sponsor the construction of a tower near the highway so that visitors could view the lines from a safe distance and still experience the power and mystery of these ancient relics. By the time Maria Reiche died at ninety-five, she was hailed as a national treasure herself and known as "The Lady of the Lines." The Peruvian president Alberto K. Fujimori even suggested that the Nazca lines should be renamed the Reiche lines. Today, the Nazca airport and over fifty schools in Peru are named after Maria Reiche.

A two-mile-long trapezoid at Nazca. Other geometric figures include squares, spirals, and triangles. Some theorists have suggested that the trapezoids resemble modern-day runways for aircrafts.

An elongated skull, excavated from the necropolis at Paracas, Peru. Many of the elongated skulls discovered in Peru are believed to be almost three thousand years old.

and wood, and they would put them at the end of the airstrip to try to attract the planes to come out of the sky and bring the cargo. And this is why we call it a cargo cult. With Nazca, we can see how a cargo cult could have developed there after the extraterrestrials who had been using it as some kind of prehistoric spaceport or airport left.

Zecharia Sitchin, an expert scholar in the history of the Sumerian culture, theorized that the Anunnaki—the gods of the ancient Sumerians—were extraterrestrials. The Anunnaki came to Nazca from Sumer, from ancient India, from Mount Meru, maybe even from the moon right to Nazca. And they were landing. They were unloading their cargo, food, clothing, high-tech objects, and tools for quarrying and working stone. This was the heyday of Nazca culture, when the Anunnaki were using Nazca as a spaceport. And then they left. The people at Nazca wanted them to come back, so they began making these symbols, creating more airstrips, hoping that the gods would return.

Recent studies at Nazca by Japanese archaeologists have indicated that there were at least four different cultures making different lines, figures, and trapezoids throughout the Nazca area. This shows that Nazca was not created by one culture at one time, but was an ongoing development for centuries, even thousands of years. The one thing that unites all the designs is that they are made to be viewed from the sky. Without an aerial view of the complex geometric designs, they make no sense. So it would seem that all of the cultures were trying to signal some kind of sky people.

Why would the Anunnaki come to Nazca in the first place? Nazca is very well situated for flight routes, particularly those that cross the Pacific Ocean. And, from Nazca, you can easily reach the Altiplano—the high plateau in Peru and Bolivia—and access areas like Tiahuanaco and Lake Titicaca. The Nazca lines that extend hundreds of miles toward those regions indicate that once you arrived in Nazca with your airship, the lines themselves directed you farther east into the Andes.

The Nazca area of Peru, along with regions just south of it called Paracas and Ica, are also the areas where archaeologists have discovered many strange elongated skulls. Similar elongated skulls have also been found at Tiahuanaco and Puma Punku. So these are the same people, whoever they were; they had elongated skulls, they were on the coast of Peru, and they were in the Andes. This elongation is an unusual cranial deformation. We don't know whether it is natural or was caused by intentional intervention, like cranial binding.

Cultures around the world going back to at least 3000 BC bound and compressed infants' skulls to force them to grow into an elongated shape. The Olmec did this. It was done in Peru. It was done on remote islands in the Pacific, like Vanuatu. It was done in Africa, in the Congo. The Kurds of northern Iraq did this. Skeletons found in Malta had elongated heads. The ancient Egyptians did it. There is

A proto-Nazca elongated skull, circa 200–100 BC.

a bust of the daughter of Akhenaten and Nefertiti, the famous pharaoh and queen of the Aten period of Egypt, and she clearly has this elongated head.

This is a mystery to archaeologists. We don't know why ancient people did this. Were they possibly trying to imitate extraterrestrials who normally looked like this? Because when we think of people with these elongated heads, we should remember that the Anunnaki were described as these giants with elongated heads. Or had they just found a way to elongate a human skull and thus double the brain capacity of a person?

And why would they do that? Were they trying to make people more psychic? Give them stronger mental abilities or something like that? What's really strange is that this is found all over the world. I mean, this is something that had to be learned, something that was taught to them.

Also in Peru we find the Ica stones. The Ica stones are thousands of stones of various sizes—some as small as a baseball; others much larger, sort of medium-size boulders—that were allegedly discovered in an area around Ica, Peru, which is south of Lima along the coastal desert going toward the famous Nazca glyphs. Each of these stones is inscribed with unusual scenes—people interacting with what seem to be prehistoric animals, or people looking

An Egyptian bas-relief portraying Akhenaten with his wife, Nefertiti, and their two daughters. Their elongated skulls are clearly visible, especially those of the two daughters who are not wearing headdresses.

A few of the controversial Ica stones. By the 1970s, Dr. Cabrera had collected more than eleven thousand specimens of the stones. In 1996, he opened his museum dedicated to showcasing them and their incredible imagery, such as what appears to be a telescope (*bottom center*).

through telescopes, for example. Some of the Ica stones seem to be strange maps of some of the world before ours.

The stones were sold to a wealthy doctor named Javier Cabrera. I met him a number of times in Peru. He created a museum for his stones. Dr. Cabrera even thought that one of the stones was in fact a map of Mars. Some of the Ica stones seem to depict ancient surgeries taking place—doctors opening people up and taking out their hearts. Dr. Cabrera believed they were depicting heart transplants and other kinds of sophisticated medical operations. The actions that are depicted on the Ica stones are so sophisticated, it seems impossible that ancient people were doing anything like this. Therefore, if the Ica stones are genuine, it would seem to be that this is medical knowledge coming from some advanced civilization of extraterrestrials.

To say the least, the Ica stones are very, very controversial. Mainstream archaeologists don't acknowledge them as genuine ancient artifacts. In fact, some accuse Dr. Cabrera of creating a gigantic hoax, but that would be fairly difficult, as there are thousands of these stones. Some people say that some are real, while some are fake. We don't really know. They can be seen today in a private museum in Ica, Peru, even though Dr. Cabrera passed away some years ago. What we do know is that the Ica stones were found near the Nazca lines. And it would seem that there is some connection between the Ica stones and the Nazca lines.

GIORGIO A. TSOUKALOS

THE GREAT PUZZLE OF PUMA PUNKU

If you were to ask researcher and publisher Giorgio A. Tsoukalos what places hold the most compelling evidence of extraterrestrial contact in our ancient past, he'd tell you that Puma Punku, near the western border of Bolivia, is on the top of his list. Tsoukalos has visited this fascinating and mysterious location many times, collecting data, logging measurements, and developing his own theory on who—or what—built and destroyed the stone structures at the ancient site known as Puma Punku.

The most tangible evidence that we have regarding possible extraterrestrial technology is, in my opinion, the stone-cutting techniques of some ancient civilizations. Because in some instances, we ourselves today would have great difficulty replicating what our ancestors allegedly accomplished with stonemasonry. Puma Punku is such a prime example.

In 1549, while searching for the capital of the Inca Empire, Pedro Cieza de León and his Spanish conquistadors discovered the ruins of what looked like a massive temple complex at what is now called Tiahuanaco (also known as Tiwanaku). Mainstream archaeologists suggest these ruins were once the center of the Tiahuanaco civilization, but little is known about the forty thousand or so people who lived here or the structures they left behind.

Of special interest are the walls of Tiahuanaco's large courtyard, which feature numerous carved stone faces that may suggest those of extraterrestrial visitors. But located just a half mile away from the temple at Tiahuanaco lie the ruins of what is thought to be yet another temple complex, the mysterious site known as Puma Punku, "The Gateway of the Puma." The name was given by the local Aymara people, who found

The Ponce Stela (*left*), a monolithic statue in the Temple of Kalasasaya at Tiahuanaco. The Ponce Stela is visible through the main door of Kalasasaya as seen from the subterranean temple. The walls of the subterranean temple are covered with 194 carvings of faces, each one different from the next.

artifacts at the site depicting warriors wearing masks made of puma skulls. But what was it? A temple? A meeting place? Some elaborate monument? All of these possibilities have been suggested, but to this day no one knows just what this place was, who built it, or exactly how old it really is.

Puma Punku is located in the highlands of the Bolivian Andes. It is situated next to Lake Titicaca, the highest navigable lake in the world. The ruins we find at Puma Punku are simply extraordinary. Puma Punku defies logic and has no comparison anywhere in the world. What we have there are not only gigantic stone platforms, which at one point in time possibly all fit together, but we also have stone cuts that are highly sophisticated and that have nothing to do with anything ritualistic or with any ornamentation such as the depictions of flowers, faces, or animals, or something that has been created for the worship of the gods. Puma Punku is an anonymous site. There are no inscriptions there. No depictions of any people. In my opinion, Puma Punku is the

most mysterious site on Planet Earth, eclipsing even the pyramids at Giza.

The most prominent stones featured at Puma Punku are grey andesite and red sandstone. We find clear evidence of a machining signature at Puma Punku. How this was done remains a mystery to this day. We also find what seem to be physical impossibilities in ancient rock-cutting techniques—in Ollantaytambu, Peru, for example—where entire blocks of stone were somehow cut out of the rock face. How was the back of that block released so that the block could be taken out from the rock face? It seems that what we have here is a physical impossibility. I've talked to mining engineers and all sorts of people involved with rock cutting, and they told me that un-

Massive stone "H" blocks at Puma Punku. Each stone was cut with incredible precision, designed to interlock with the surrounding stones. The blocks fit together like a puzzle, forming load-bearing joints without the use of mortar.

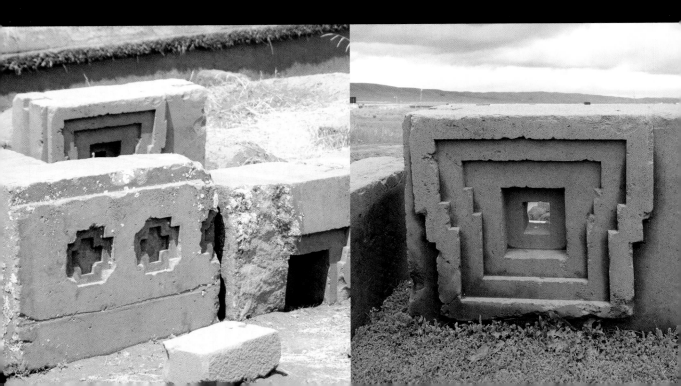

Top: Megalithic Andesite blocks at Puma Punku. On the right side of the image is a block featuring four equidistant holes carved into its corners. *Bottom left:* Precision stonework at Puma Punku. *Bottom right:* Extraordinary craftsmanship at Puma Punku.

less you have an access point where you can slide the blade behind it, you cannot do this. If modern-day engineers tell me that today we don't have an easy way of doing this, then how on Earth did our ancestors succeed in releasing the back of the block?

The reason I am convinced that sophisticated technology was utilized in cutting these ancient rocks is that if we go to a stone quarry today and look at the scope of machinery required to accomplish similar things, well, those machines are huge. They're monstrosities that not only have these big, gigantic blades to release the stone blocks from the rock face, but also need added water, because if you don't add water to the blades, then the blades will get too hot and disintegrate or melt.

At Puma Punku there's this one andesite block that has this perfect groove with holes drilled at equidistant positions. Now, it is a scientific fact that an andesite block cannot be cut with copper tools. That's just how it is. For many years, researchers have suggested that some type of laser or plasma tools were used at Puma Punku. However, through machinist and toolmaker Christopher Dunn's research, we have evidence that lasers or plasma tools—heat-related tools—were never used on these blocks. However, what we do find is a surface that might have been achieved with a type of diamond saw or diamond mill. Anyone who has ever been to Puma Punku marvels at the fact that when you touch the cut rocks, their surface is extremely fine. It's almost like touching a bathroom mirror—that is how fine and perfect the surfaces are at Puma Punku. The mainstream archaeology explanation that all of this was accomplished with obsidian or with chicken bones doesn't hold up.

Another question we have to ask ourselves is, How were these giant platforms moved from point A to point B? According to some scholars, the quarries for these stones were as far away as eighty miles. Some have suggested that these stone blocks were transported with the help of wooden rollers. But what nobody talks about is the fact that Tiahuanaco is situated at an altitude of 12,800 feet, which means we are above the natural tree line.

No trees ever grew in that area, meaning no trees were cut down there to use as wooden rollers. The wooden-roller theory falls away.

On Wikipedia you can read that Puma Punku was built between AD 536 and AD 600. But, if you ask somebody like me, Puma Punku and Tiahuanaco might date back as far as 12,000 BC—about 14,000 years ago. And the idea that a precivilization existed before our recorded history is something that ancient astronaut theorists have tried to prove for a very long time—that our history dates back much further than what we have been taught.

Puma Punku and Tiahuanaco might date back as far as 12,000 BC.

When Dr. Arthur Posnansky, an eminent archaeologist, looked at Tiahuanaco, he determined the symbols that are carved on many of the monuments are part of a calendar. When he sat down to calculate the age of the monuments based on that calendar, he came up with a number that is incredibly old, at least ten thousand years. One of the results that he calculated actually went back seventeen thousand years. So we have a monument that for all intents and purposes was determined, through its own calendar, to be seventeen thousand years old. Mainstream archaeologists consider those calculations false. They think that he might have made a mistake or that the symbols themselves contained mistakes essentially indicating that our ancestors didn't know what they carved into the rock. I disagree with that notion, because our ancestors were as smart as we are today, intellectually speaking. The only variation is that they had a difference in comprehension of technology. In other words, their technological frame of reference was more primitive than ours today.

Today, with ground-penetrating radar, researchers have actually determined that there are more blocks, and some of these blocks are now being excavated at a depth of twelve feet. This means there is a lot of soil that had to have been built up for everything to disappear. The idea is that

GOLD FLYERS

The dense jungles and rugged mountains of Colombia contain a vast number of archaeological sites. Many treasure hunters believe the legendary city of gold, El Dorado, lies hidden there, somewhere beneath a thick canopy of trees. While the mythical metropolis has yet to be discovered, early in the twentieth century tomb raiders searching along the Magdalena River stumbled upon a grave site that mainstream archaeologists date back to a pre-Columbian civilization known as the Quimbaya (Tolima). The Quimbaya were famous for their gold and metalwork.

Among the objects the tomb raiders found were thousands of small, two- to three-inch solid gold figurines, intricately and precisely carved. Though many of the figurines represented local insects and wildlife, a handful stood out for their remarkable resemblance, in minute detail, to modern aircraft—demonstrating that the Quimbaya understood the principles of flight. In 1996, German aviation enthusiasts and model builders Dr. Algund Eenboom and Peter Belting successfully built and flew remote-controlled scale models of two of the gold flyers, adding only landing gear and an engine—demonstrating without a doubt that the gold Quimbaya flyers are aerodynamically sound.

How could our ancestors—who lived thousands of years before aerospace engineering—have so accurately depicted airplanes? Could they have observed such craft firsthand? Is it possible that our ancestors witnessed aircraft in flight, similar to our modern planes, piloted by extraterrestrial beings?

the reason we can find blocks and structures that are five, six, and ten feet underground is that at some point some type of a cataclysm happened that washed over everything and thus we have that thick soil level above those structures.

So who built Puma Punku? According to the native Aymara people, it was not them. When you ask them who built it, they point to the sky and say it was *los dioses:* the gods. So then we have what is called living mythology, in which people still alive today tell us exactly how some of these things came about. The Aymara themselves say that they had no hand in building Puma Punku. According to oral traditions of the Aymara, Tiahuanaco was built as a place of pilgrimage for significant events that took place at Puma Punku. What were these significant events? According to the traditions, people descended from the sky and jump-started civilization in that region of the world. Yet when we hear stories like this, we look the other way and say, *Oh, come on. It's nothing else but fantasy.*

When the first Spanish chroniclers appeared on the scene, and they asked the locals "Who built Puma Punku?," the locals told of a legend that Puma Punku was built in a single night by the gods. When you look at the complex that we find today, though, it's very hard to believe that any of this was built in one night. Again, what we have here is mythology. But any type of mythology is rooted in some type of truth. So we have to figure out what the truth is behind Puma Punku.

The locals told of a legend that Puma Punku was built in a single night by the gods.

Calendar calculations of some of the glyphs found at Tiahuanaco suggest that Tiahuanaco may have been built because of what may have happened at Puma Punku before. And Tiahuanaco is nothing else but a place of pilgrimage for people to congregate and remember the time when something significant happened at Puma Punku. In my opinion, the thing that was significant about it was an extraterrestrial visit by ancient aliens in the remote past that our ancestors witnessed firsthand.

I think that Puma Punku is the only site on Planet Earth that may have been built directly by extraterrestrials. Even though I wouldn't be surprised if the extraterrestrials commissioned the Aymara to help them in their undertaking. I say this because I don't think the extraterrestrials ever got their hands dirty. They simply showed our ancestors how to use their machines. To be clear, the pyramids were built by human beings. In fact, I think that *all* of the ancient monuments were built by human beings. But the extraterrestrials shared their engineering knowledge with our ancestors. Puma Punku was a type of base camp from which they sent out their craft in order to explore, for example, the Americas. Bear in mind that we also have stories of Viracocha or Kukulcan or Quetzalcoatl—the winged serpent—arriving at Lake Titicaca, which is considered to be a navel of the world. And a navel of the world in ancient times was considered to be a place where life originated. Delphi, Greece, is considered another such navel.

Today, Puma Punku is in ruins. That means there was a point in time when Puma Punku was complete. So what happened? Is it possible that some type of a cataclysmic event destroyed Puma Punku? Or was it disassembled on purpose? As with any visit, or any project, the time arrives when it is finished. And that is why some of these contacts ended—because the extraterrestrials went on to different places. I also speculate that Puma Punku was deliberately destroyed by its original builders, the extraterrestrials, right before they decided to leave Planet Earth and go on to their next mission.

JASON MARTELL

THE CRADLE OF ALIEN CIVILIZATION

For nearly two decades, Jason Martell has been one of the leading researchers and lecturers specializing in ancient civilization technologies. Lecturing throughout the world, Martell has dedicated his studies to ancient artifacts, Planet X, ancient astronauts, and the structures on Mars.

While studying the anomalies of the planet Mars, Martell began a quest to learn about the oldest-known culture on Earth, the Sumerian culture, and the secrets that their cuneiform writing may hold about our extraterrestrial origins.

The first recorded civilization that we have on the books of antiquity is Sumer, which is in modern-day southern Iraq. Right out of the Stone Age, the Sumerian culture comes into existence and they create over one hundred of the "firsts" needed for a modern civilization: schools, astronomy, medicine, agriculture, and so on. Many of the pinnacle developments that we use today sprung up overnight in southern Iraq. We see this technology, spawned in ancient Iraq, being disseminated through all of the other Middle Eastern cultures and into South America as well.

How did this take place if there weren't any transoceanic cultures at that time? Maybe as the ancient people tell us, their gods were possibly also extraterrestrials and would've had very easy global access to all the civilizations.

What's interesting about the Sumerian culture is that they've left us artifacts and stone tablets that still exist today. Their written language, cuneiform script, was recorded in clay. Zecharia Sitchin was a linguist who not only translated Sumerian cuneiform writings, but also looked at other cultures, saw how certain words were shared, and then validated them as accurate linguistic translations. Sitchin really took the next step in making the connections between Sumer and other cultures, and not just by showing the translation of a word or a phrase. He spent fifty years doing research into these topics.

Sitchin was also one of the scholars to pioneer the idea that the Sume-

CUNEIFORM

The oldest writing system in the world, cuneiform—wedge-shaped writing—was developed by the Sumerians but used by all of the great Mesopotamian civilizations, from the Assyrians to the Babylonians. Clay tablets were the ideal medium for everyday cuneiform records such as bills and inventories, but cuneiform was also carved into stone at temples and monuments.

rian gods, the Anunnaki, were flesh-and-blood beings, basing his conclusions on the Sumerians' cuneiform writings, which very clearly describe a race of beings who lived among them and whom they described as being their gods.

If you were to ask an ancient Sumerian, "How is it that you know so much about astronomy and mathematics?" they'd have said, "Everything we know we were taught by the Anunnaki," meaning those who come from heaven to Earth. The Sumerians were very clear in diagramming all of the known planets in our solar system accurately. However, they included an additional planet, which they called Nibiru and identified it as the home planet of the Anunnaki.

Sumerian depictions of the Anunnaki always show them as descending from the skies in a winged disk. Why a winged disk? Well, ancient humans didn't understand technology the way we do today. So after seeing a being like this coming down from the heavens in some type of craft, they gave the craft wings to show that it had the power of flight. It means they were witnessing the power of flight.

The Anunnaki are said to have originally arrived on Earth 450,000 years ago. They came seeking gold and precious elements to repair their planet's dwindling atmosphere. They explained to the Sumerians that through their own rise to a technological culture, they damaged their atmosphere—but found that they could repair it by spraying fine particulates of gold into the atmosphere. Sitchin translated ancient Sumerian tablets that describe the Anunnaki using Mars as a

LOST WRITINGS OF THE ANCIENTS

On the east bank of the Tigris River, near the modern city of Mosul, Iraq, lie the ruins of the ancient city of Nineveh. Historians call this part of the world the "cradle of civilization" because it was home to the Sumerians, an advanced civilization that originally inhabited Mesopotamia from approximately 3000 to 4000 BC. The ancient Sumerians created the first-known form of writing, called cuneiform, consisting of shapes and symbols inscribed on clay tablets or carved into stone. For three millennia, the cuneiform writing system was used by ancient peoples. But by the second century AD, the script had become extinct, and all knowledge of how to read it would be lost for thousands of years.

It was in the ruins of Nineveh that archaeologists discovered great archives of as many as thirty thousand of these cuneiform clay tablets. Like many ancient cultures, the Sumerians devoted their writing to accounts of the creation of Earth and humankind. But what has puzzled archaeologists for years were the stories the Sumerians wrote about their gods, a tribe of beings they called the "Anunnaki." The Sumerians believed these "gods" had descended from the sky to Earth long before the Sumerians had arrived in Nineveh.

A decade after the discovery of the trove of tablets, archaeologists stumbled upon another find that would shock the world: the ruins of the legendary Sumerian capital city of Ur. For centuries, this city was thought to have been a myth. But at this site, scientists discovered the great Ziggurat of Ur, a pyramid-shaped structure over one hundred feet high that was said to have been the administrative center of the city. The cuneiform tablets found at this site revealed an actual ancient Sumerian culture that was versed in agriculture, science, medicine, mathematics, kingship, laws, courts, judges, and schools. Yet, of the half million to two million cuneiform tablets that have been excavated in modern times, only about thirty thousand to one hundred thousand have been read or published. Millions of tablets wait to reveal their secrets. Could it be that here, in the ancient cuneiform texts, we will find further evidence of aliens coming to Earth and sharing their extensive knowledge?

way station in transporting gold from Earth to Nibiru. And there are descriptions of a large monument of an Anunnaki face being built on Mars—which still exists today as the face on Mars.

When the Anunnaki first landed here on Earth, some were assigned to dig canals and others to work in mining. Others were assigned to do ship building and things at sea. After about forty or fifty years, the Anunnaki who were building the canals and doing the mining on Earth started to revolt. These gods said, *Listen, this work is too much of a laborious task for us. We would like to create a slave race fashioned from the hominoid being that lives here naturally, that would do the work for us.* And that's exactly what the Sumerian texts tell us: human beings were created to assist the gods in doing their work.

It's an interesting similarity that the Sumerians describe the Anunnaki coming here and creating us in their image, just as the Bible says God did with Adam and Eve, but with the Anunnaki, it's for a specific purpose—to mine gold for them. And if we think about our obsession with gold today, people have only to hold gold and they get excited, not to mention gold's monetary value in our current financial structure. Maybe we're even genetically programmed to not only mine the gold, but to really like the gold.

Sumerian legends describe how two Anunnaki scientists created us in their image, how they genetically engineered the first human being. Interestingly, our DNA contains a bunch of "junk DNA." And we haven't been able to determine what this is possibly used for. Humans' genetic structure seems to have been patched together, spliced here, moved there. It's a very disorganized system, in which we have actual genetic leftover material. So, many theories suggest that "junk DNA" could be leftover extraterrestrial material.

Mainstream science tries to explain human evolution by looking at fossil records of different skulls and bones and drawing a connection between us and the Neanderthal or the Australopithecus, whom we know was evolving here on Earth. But they haven't been able to find what they call the missing link, some type of species that actually connects us to the Neanderthal. Because they are in no way us. They're big boned; they're

Top: Assyrian winged deities (Anunnaki) flank the Tree of Life in an Assyrian relief circa 865 BC, from the Palace of King Ashurnasirpal in the ancient city of Nimrud, Iraq. Bottom: Eighth century BC Assyrian reliefs of a winged god and a jaguar-headed god, also from the Palace of King Ashurnasirpal in the ancient city of Nimrud, Iraq.

full of hair. If we were born into the wild, we would burn from the sun, we would get cut by leaves and branches—somehow along the way, there was a genetic intervention from the Neanderthal to us.

When we look at the Enuma Elish, the Babylonian creation epic written in Sumerian cuneiform, we see a very interesting description of how the first man was created. When we look at the pictogram that accompanies the Enuma Elish, we see a scene of the chief Anunnaki scientist, Ninhursag, holding up the atom. And, as a backdrop, we see what appear to be vases or tubes on a shelf. Could this be the first sign of an in vitro fertilization?

An ancient cuneiform star map excavated from the seventh century BC Library of Ashurbanipal in the ruins of Nineveh, Iraq. The oldest surviving royal library in the world, it comprises more than thirty thousand cuneiform texts.

The Enuma Elish also recounts a war breaking out among the Anunnaki, and describes the god Marduk returning to Jupiter. This could be partly why they kept such accurate astronomical data, perhaps for tracking this exiting and returning of their god. The Babylonians were very astute astronomers. They built structures that allowed them to do very specific measurements of the sky, and recorded this as sacred information, sometimes over hundreds or even thousands of years.

But they aren't the only ones. It turns out that all over the planet, we have stone edifices where there have been clear observations that allow for astronomical movements to have been tracked. A lot of these places around the world that were used for astronomical observations could have been set up for a specific reason why they were watching the sky. It could be that they were aware of a larger cycle of time that talked about the return of certain gods that would be coming to Earth. And it seems that every culture around the world has a similar line of watching the heavens for key markers of changes, to know when something might predict the return of their gods.

Maybe there's a deeper layer of our history that we can discover by unearthing some of these artifacts and seeing that there is a technological part of our history we still have yet to uncover. And if we look at all the other ancient cultures—the Mayans, the Inca, the Egyptians—they all have this knowledge of a celestial-based time system. A lot of information that we hold as sacred mythological tales could in fact be data describing a time when humans interacted with living gods, what we would today call extraterrestrials.

There are many similarities in mythologies around the world that speak of a time when gods lived among their people. We look at it now as simply mythology. But every culture around the world went to great lengths to inscribe hieroglyphs and create huge monuments dedicated to their gods, which talk about a time when their gods were actually here. Many of the biblical stories that take place in what were once considered mythical locations, such as the ancient city of Ur, have been discovered by archaeologists and confirmed as real. And when they excavated the ancient city of Ur they found unbelievable artifacts, like the flood tablet, which is one of the earliest recorded tellings of a great deluge, of the Flood.

Mythological tales could in fact be data describing a time when humans interacted with living gods.

When we analyze the Sumerian myths about the Anunnaki, we really need to consider them in that light. Everything else the Sumerians left us our science has confirmed is accurate—from mathematics and astronomical information to laws, courts, and judges. Unfortunately, though, when they talk about the Anunnaki, science still has a problem crossing that line that extraterrestrials exist.

DAVID HATCHER CHILDRESS

TEMPLES OF BLOOD AND GOLD

The ancient Mayan civilization dominated present-day Central America for over two thousand years. Regarded by scholars as one of the most sophisticated and complex civilizations in the ancient world, Mayan triumphs included numerous scientific achievements in agriculture, engineering, and astronomy as well as advanced mythology, language, and religious culture. Without metal tools, the wheel, or pack animals, the Mayans built cities like Palenque, Copán, Tikal, and Calakmul.

David Childress has written extensively about his travels through the ancient Mayan kingdoms and shares details on the many clues the Mayans left behind that suggest that their origin—and destiny—had been plotted by otherworldly forces.

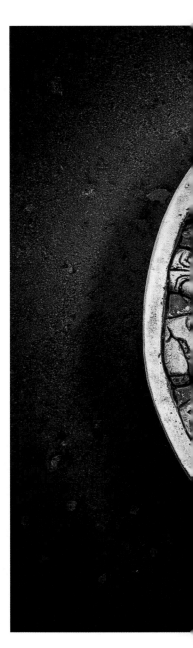

Building up to the year 2012, there was a lot of renewed interest in and excitement about the Mayan calendar system. People were tuning in to the idea that the Mayans and other ancient civilizations had knowledge of periodic cataclysms and of vast cosmic cycles. Mayan mythology says that there have been four or five worlds before our own. And each one is annihilated in a cataclysmic upheaval that destroys civilization, destroys animals, and creates fossils. And then, the world is begun anew.

Mainstream scientists tell us that, basically, the modern human civilization started in the Stone Age. Somehow we lived in caves and ended up here. They just draw a straight line from there to modern man. But the evidence shows something different, which is that the development of civilization has been a roller coaster of ups and downs: of ages of enlightenment, golden ages, then a dark age, and an age where science and civilization have been lost. There is evidence, too, that ancient civilizations were much more advanced than we give them credit for.

For example, there are Mayan frescos, Toltec statues, and Olmec statues that depict figures holding objects we can't identify. Sometimes they've got things in their mouths that

The Mayan Calendar comprises *three* cyclical calendars: The Long Count (the astronomical calendar, which tracks a cycle approximately 2,880,000 days long), the Tzolkin (the 260-day divine calendar), and the Haab (the 365-day civil calendar). The calendar dates back to at least the fifth century BC.

look like breathing apparatuses, or oddball devices in their hands that could be laser pistols or antigravity beam devices, or something like that. We assume that because they're primitive people they couldn't have had high-tech devices. We already possess many similar advanced technologies. So the idea that some of the Mayan and Toltec kings were running around with special breathing apparatuses, even listening devices and radio devices in their ears, in my mind there's no reason they couldn't have had those things, too. And they would've come from extraterrestrials or else some other very high-tech civilization with all kinds of electronic devices, power saws, airships, and so on.

At the ancient Mayan city of Palenque was a tomb that was discovered in the 1950s. And inside this tomb was a sarcophagus. The lid of the sarcophagus is very highly decorated and depicts the Mayan king Lord Pakal. In the picture he's doing some really unusual things. He's sitting in a chair. He seems to be operating devices. There's something like a rocket plume underneath him. Because our own age of rockets had only just begun in the 1960s, when Erich von Däniken looked at that lid, he saw a Mayan king in a rocket ship. And that guy was returning to the stars, going back into space. It was an exciting interpretation, and it was one of the main things in *Chariots of the Gods*. When other people looked at that lid and read von Däniken's explanation, they had to agree

SECRETS IN STONE

A stone carving discovered in the ruins at Tikal, an ancient Mayan city (dating back to 400 BC) in Guatemala, strongly resembles a modern astronaut wearing a space helmet.

with him and thought, *Yeah. This is an interesting explanation for this lid and Lord Pakal.*

At the ruins of Copán in Honduras, which was one of the most important Mayan cities, there are strange statues that seem to have all these extra appendages, antennas coming out of their heads, other kinds of wires, and even levers that are part of these creatures. And you have to wonder, *Is this just some weird monster with all kinds of levers coming out of him? Or is this maybe some kind of a robot?*

There are also structures in the region that suggest that Mayan stories about past ages may be true. The Qhapaq Nan, the famous Inca road system, was actually developed on an earlier road system. That road system goes for thousands of miles through the Andes. It goes through Chile and parts of Argentina, through Peru and Bolivia, and into Ecuador and Colombia. The road system passes through high mountains, deserts, and jungles. There are tunnels cut through solid rock. There are bridges that extend over chasms in the Andes. Some of these had to be very elaborate rope bridges. But others were megalithic bridges made of stone, such as the megalithic bridge at Chavin, which is gone today. The construction of such an extensive road system would have required surveying the land it crossed, with its extreme environments of high mountains, deserts, and jungles. There would had to have been aerial surveys of this land. We couldn't build such a road system today without aerial surveys. It would seem that only an advanced civilization could have conceived of and constructed this amazing road system.

When the Spanish first conquered Peru, they—just like tourists today—were completely amazed at the gigantic blocks around Cusco, Sacsayhuaman, and Lake Titicaca. They asked the Inca people who had built these amazing structures. The Inca themselves admitted that they had not built all of them. In fact, they had elaborate legends of traveling throughout Peru through tunnel systems already in place deep in the earth, emerging on an island in Lake Titicaca, and then coming to Cusco to find another system of tunnels, ancient mines, and structures—and then taking over what was to become the Inca Empire.

Unfortunately, throughout our history, humankind has amassed giant armies, invaded other civilizations, and destroyed everything they could find. They tore down temples if they could. The Spanish did exactly this in Central and South America. They destroyed many of the ancient temples and structures they found there. They destroyed every manuscript they could get a hold of. Thousands of Mayan codices were burned. We'll never know what they said. With the loss of those libraries we lost an irreplaceable connection to the past: what happened in the past, who we are, what our history is. With the destruction of those libraries, we may well have lost our connection to the gods, the extraterrestrials of the past, such as the Mayan god known as the feathered serpent.

The whole mythology of the feathered serpent sky god, Kukulcan or Quetzalcoatl, is very powerful and important within Mesoamerican cultures, especially the Mayan and Aztec cultures. The Toltec also worshipped Quetzalcoatl. In fact, a number of Toltec kings took on the name Quetzalcoatl. Mesoamerican mythology tells us that after

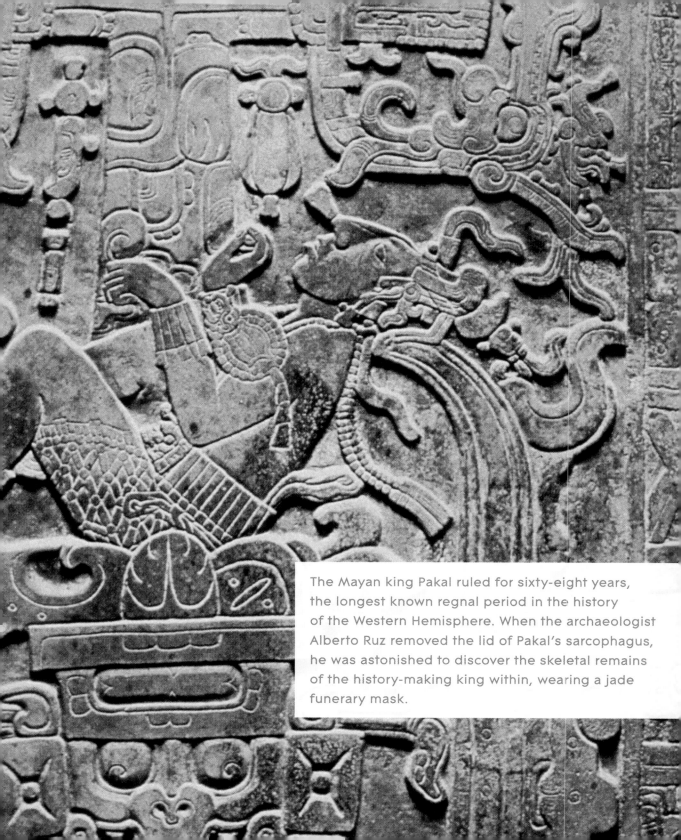

The Mayan king Pakal ruled for sixty-eight years, the longest known regnal period in the history of the Western Hemisphere. When the archaeologist Alberto Ruz removed the lid of Pakal's sarcophagus, he was astonished to discover the skeletal remains of the history-making king within, wearing a jade funerary mask.

THE TOMB OF THE PALENQUE ASTRONAUT

Deep in the jungle of Chiapas, Mexico, amid a tangle of fragrant cedar, mahogany, and sapodilla trees, rises one of the great Mayan step pyramids: the Temple of the Inscriptions. The funerary monument of the great Mayan king Lord Pakal, it is the largest pyramid at the ruins of Palenque, the Mayan city over which Pakal ruled for a commanding sixty-eight years. Though Spanish explorers and later archaeologists were aware of the abandoned city and its imposing palace, temples, and courtyards of gray stone as early as the sixteenth century, it wasn't until 1952 that Mexican archaeologist Alberto Ruz would discover the astonishing secret at the heart of the Temple of the Inscriptions.

Having ascended to the graceful temple atop the pyramid, Ruz noticed what appeared to be a sort of trapdoor inset in the temple's floor. After his crew removed the heavy stone slab, they were shocked to discover what appeared to be a stairway leading down into the interior of the pyramid. Obstructed by rubble, the stairway would not be cleared for another two years.

Ruz's patience would pay off, however—for once the stairway was cleared he found that it led to a secret chamber deep underground, a room unlike any other in the realm of Mesoamerican pyramids. Icicle-shaped stalactites dripped perilously from the ceiling, and sharp stalagmites rose menacingly from its floor.

And at the heart of this sepulchral chamber, hidden from sight for over one thousand years, stood the massive sarcophagus of King Pakal, sealed with an incredibly heavy, incredibly intricate, carved lid. The sarcophagus lid

depicts Pakal within a capsulelike object, reclining in a cocoonlike seat, manipulating what appears to be a set of controls with one hand while seemingly dialing a piece of equipment with the other. The heel of his left foot rests on what looks like a pedal. He has on what looks like a face mask, with an apparatus of some type emerging from his mouth. Affixed to his chest appears to be some form of monitoring unit. From what looks to be an engine beneath the capsule, flames erupt.

Taken together, the details of the lid create an unshakable portrait of a man—or being—who is, in posture and outfit, remarkably, startlingly, like one of our own astronauts. In fact, its eerie similarity to a twenty-first-century space voyager has earned it the nickname by which it is now commonly known: the Palenque Astronaut. But the Palenque Astronaut is only one of countless mysteries the Mayans left behind, along with other Mesoamerican cultures—from eerily futuristic statues to vast and complex tunnel systems.

cataclysms, the sky gods would bring civilization and its tools back to the various people all over the world. And they would then show humans the arts of metallurgy, agriculture, and architecture.

In the Yucatán region of Mexico, people have claimed to have seen the lost Golden Books of the Maya in certain ruins, but that their existence must be kept secret. And there are reasons to keep this a secret. For people in Central and South American countries, finding a treasure trove of gold tablets and statues would probably land you in big trouble. The government would seize it from you and probably put you in prison. I believe that because of this, many finds are deliberately kept secret by their discoverers. When you think about it, in a world of cyclical cataclysms, of ancient wars in which civilizations have come and gone, it makes sense that people would create underground repositories for information, and that ancient aliens would stash valuable artifacts or books—written in gold, which does not decay—in a safe place to preserve them for history. It all makes sense to me.

On a number of expeditions to remote areas of South America, I've encountered tunnels like the ones de-

A feathered serpent head adorns the Temple of Quetzalcoatl at Teotihuacan, Mexico (*top*), while a fierce feathered serpent guards the base of the Temple of Kukulcan at Chichen Itza, Mexico (*bottom*).

scribed by the Inca. I've walked through a few of them in Brazil and in Bolivia. At Sacsayhuaman in Peru, there are said to be entrances to a bizarre underground tunnel system that runs for thousands of miles through the Andes.

Maybe the most mysterious underground network is the Tayos Cave system in the mountain jungles of eastern Ecuador. This part of Ecuador is very remote and dangerous to reach. Back in the early 1970s, several Ecuadorians contacted Erich von Däniken and told him that they could take him there, and that inside the caves he would find alien artifacts, gold tablets, copper tablets, and mysterious statues. He went and ended up writing his third book, *The Gold of the Gods,* largely about the experience and all the things he had seen there, which were just as the Ecuadorians had promised. In the mid-1970s, a British Special Forces expedition explored Tayos, as did Neil Armstrong, the first person to walk on the moon. Many people were fascinated by the stories around Tayos.

One of the most fascinating stories related to the Tayos caves is the story of the Crespi collection, a collection of metal and stone artifacts in the care of a priest, Father Crespi, who lived in Cuenca, Ecuador. He had all of these artifacts, plus strange gold tablets and similar items, to what was believed to be in the Tayos caves. Both collections have disappeared. I went to Cuenca one time to try to track down that collection from Father Crespi after he passed away in 1982. I talked to priests there who said that they didn't know where the collection went, that those artifacts had vanished, but that photographs of them still existed. Those artifacts may well have come from the Tayos caves.

At Sacsayhuaman there are said to be entrances to a tunnel system that runs for thousands of miles through the Andes.

The Tayos caves are said to connect with a vast underground tunnel system that connects Peru, Chile, Bolivia, and Brazil. The Inca were said to know about the entrances to some of these secret tunnels. One of the popular stories in Peru is that when the Inca realized that the Spanish were coming, they took the treasure from the Temple of the Sun in Cusco and hid it all. Peruvians say the Inca hid it either in that hidden tunnel system, under Sacsayhuaman, or in a secret city in the mountain jungles, known as Paititi, which is the ultimate lost city of the Inca. And sometimes it, too, is said to be reached by a secret tunnel.

The Mayans themselves have very intriguing legends of an underground world, called Xibalba. Just recently, archaeologists working at Tzibichen in the Yucatán uncovered a series of man-made rooms underground, a cave system connected by underground roads. Archaeologists now believe that what they found is what the Mayans thought was the entrance to the legendary underground world that features prominently in the Popol Vuh.

There's also the mystery of the disappearance of many of the Mayans—hundreds of cities in Guatemala and Mexico were simply deserted, and we don't know why. The Mayans in the Petén jungles of the Yucatán abandoned their cities and, to a large extent, vanished. We don't really know what happened to them or where they went. Throughout history, other civilizations have also essentially vanished for no discernible reason. We have this with the Anasazi, in the southwest of the United States; people like the Etruscans in Italy; the people who were building Carnac in Brittany, and even Stonehenge in England; and many of the megaliths around the world—we don't know who they were. And even archaeologists will admit, *Yeah, it's not the people who live in Brittany or England today who built those things.* So mass disappearances—whole areas just completely depopulated—have happened; I mean, we know it. And the exact causes for this remain a mystery.

So you have to ask, Where did they all go? Regarding the Mayans, Erich von Däniken suggested they returned to the stars. The Mayan monuments at Tikal are known to be aligned to the Pleiades cluster. And so we must ask

The Pleiades star system. Cultures around the world have known of the Pleiades since antiquity—the Babylonians called the system "the star of stars." The earliest known depiction of the Pleiades is on the circa 1600 BC Nebra Sky Disc, a Bronze Age artifact discovered in Germany, which also features the oldest concrete depiction of the cosmos worldwide.

ourselves whether the Pleiades was some important place for the Mayans, and whether they had perhaps come from the Pleiades. Then you have to wonder: Did these Mayans actually somehow return to the Pleiades, where they had come from?

GIORGIO A. TSOUKALOS

THE MEGALITHS

What compelled ancient man to move colossal stones, in some cases weighing thousands of pounds, to build remarkably similar stone monuments all around the world? Ancient astronaut theorist Giorgio A. Tsoukalos has studied monoliths and megalithic sites around the globe and offers his theory on how ancient people achieved extraordinary feats of construction without advanced tools or technology.

Is it possible that ancient megaliths have an extraterrestrial connection we have yet to confirm?

MEGALITHS WORLDWIDE

The main reason ancient astronauts may have given technological tools to our ancestors was to leave messages for the future. A message that would let future generations know that extraterrestrials were here in our remote past. One such message comes in the shape of megalithic structures. It defies logic that our early ancestors, with their limited technology, could have built these gigantic megalithic structures with the most gigantic stones all on their own. I think that all those ancient monuments—the really big ones, like Baalbek—were built with sophisticated technology and under the tutelage of extraterrestrials.

Many of the megalithic sites all around the world should be viewed essentially as calling cards from someone who was here in the past, a past in which extraterrestrials brought the

tools with which to build these sites and taught humankind how to use these tools. They instructed the people how to build certain things, gave them the engineering knowledge, gave them all the types of knowledge needed to build something magnificent. After they were done, the extra-terrestrials took their tools and disappeared again. That is why it is very unlikely that we'll ever find any type of tool used to build those monuments. It's like if you walked into a newly built hospital—it's very unlikely you'd be wheeled into the surgery room and the concrete mixer would still be there, left behind after construction. That concrete mixer is now at the next construction site. Apply this same concept to extraterrestrial technology.

Imagine in the not-too-distant future that we, ourselves, travel to a distant planet that has some sort of intelligent life on it. That life, technologically (though not intellectually) speaking, is primitive. What will we do? Just stand back and observe? At first yes, but then we might teach them a few things. We'll teach them mathematics; we'll teach them about the constellations, astronomy, and agriculture; we'll teach them how to make fire; and then we'll disappear again. We'll go on to the next planet with our generation starship. But fast-forward ten thousand years and on the planet we left behind, they'll have stories of "gods" descending from the sky, teaching

On the outskirts of Cusco, Peru, stand the walls of Sacsayhuaman, the remnants of an ancient Incan citadel. Built from massive stone blocks laid together without mortar, the walls are so precisely crafted that not even a piece of paper can fit between their seams.

Machu Picchu was built circa 1450 in the classical Inca style called "ashlar," which involves cutting stone blocks and fitting them together without mortar. The site's three most notable structures are the ritual stone Inti Watana, the Temple of the Sun, and the Room of the Three Windows.

the society about mathematics and scientific disciplines, and all of a sudden our once-real visit will have moved into the realm of mythology.

There is one way we could at least try to leave behind evidence that we were there, and that is to have those technologically primitive people help us build megalithic structures made out of stone that endures forever. Our idea would be that one day, ten thousand years or so in the future of that planet, somebody would stumble upon these megalithic sites and think, *Wait a second. These things are ten thousand years old. How were they built? One hundred centuries ago our people didn't even know about the wheel, so how is this possible?* At some point in our human history we received help, and that's how we, over time, developed into the magnificent society we are today.

MACHU PICCHU AND SACSAYHUAMAN

Machu Picchu is located in present-day Peru, about an hour and a half from Cusco. It's a very fascinating site—you have three different types of masonry there, three styles of construction. In style one, you find what's considered megalithic: big, gigantic stones that fit together so precisely that it's impossible to put a dollar bill between their seams. Then you have style two, with smaller stones. The stones are still fairly big in size, but not as big as in style one. And then you have masonry style three, where builders used smaller, fist-size stones. And it seems like the builders began with style one and progressed to using styles two and three.

Logic would suggest, though, that "primitive" people (technologically speaking) would start building using the *small-*

Stone blocks from the walls of Sacsayhuaman. The largest of the blocks at this site are estimated to weigh nearly two hundred tons.

est stones. Over time, as their technology and knowledge of masonry increased, they would shift to using the biggest stones, because they would be more familiar with and more knowledgeable about construction. At Machu Picchu and Sacsayhuaman, however, it seems it's the exact opposite. I mean, it makes no sense. Archaeologists agree that at Machu Picchu, the first stage was built by the pre-Inca culture, not the later Inca. When you ask the archaeologists who these pre-Inca were, you don't get a clear answer, because everyone has a different opinion. That question has not been resolved.

> *At Sacsayhuaman no mortar was used in its construction. The blocks look as if they've been molded like putty.*

One very interesting structure at Machu Picchu consists of a natural rock formation in which two rocks create an X, and in between, there is a man-made block wall. It seems as if the blocks in the wall were poured into place, as if the builders had been able to soften the stone and then pour it, and over time it hardened. And there are ancient Incan legends that suggest they did have the ability to soften stone. At Sacsayhuaman, for example, we also find these gigantic stone walls where it looks as if the stones were molded and then put into place.

At Sacsayhuaman, some of the stone blocks are so huge that you feel like an ant when standing next to them. No mortar was used in its construction style. The blocks look as if they've been molded like putty, and guess what, there is an ancient Incan legend that says these stones were molded into place. The story goes that in Peru there is a bird—the Lit-Lik—that doesn't make its nests in trees but on the side of a rock face. The bird is able to peck into the rock and create a little hole for its nest. But how is it possible for a bird to pick away at rock? Well, apparently the bird chews a type of herb, a chemical reaction takes place in its beak, and then it releases that chemical onto the stone and softens it. So I believe that this chemical process was mastered by whoever built the Sacsayhuaman wall, and that they used this stone-softening process on a much larger scale, to mold megaliths into place

GOBEKLI TEPE

Just outside the Turkish city of Urfa, a town that has been continuously populated since at least the fourth century BC and that Judaism and Islam identify as the hometown of Abraham, lies an even more ancient site, one that has roots in humankind's oldest acts of worship: Gobekli Tepe, which may just be the world's oldest—and most mysterious—temple.

Though it was in the 1960s that archaeologists first made note of the "tell"—an earthen mound created by human occupation, and then abandonment of a site— under which Gobekli Tepe would eventually be discovered, they dismissed it as a pile of stones of no significance. Thirty years later, it was a local shepherd, crossing the dusty hilltop, who noticed the tip of an unusual stone sticking out of the soil—a stone that appeared, from its sharp corners and smooth surface, to be man-made. He began to dig, eventually unearthing a sixteen-foot pillar. Its edges were precise, and rising from its center was a relief carving of a strange animal. Upon closer examination, the finely chiseled stone appeared to have been fashioned by talented stonemasons, working with advanced tools. When word of the discovery reached the scientific community, one fact became obvious: a Kurdish shepherd had stumbled upon what is perhaps the most astonishing and important archaeological discovery of modern times, one that challenges our assumptions about ancient man and raises questions about our ancestors for which mainstream science can find no definitive answers.

Gobekli Tepe—a massive complex of finely carved megalithic stones arranged in concentric circles over a vast plateau—is believed by archaeologists to be ten thousand years old. The sixteen-foot, ten-ton pillar the shepherd found was only one of many. The archaeologists excavating the site have uncovered countless T-shaped megaliths, incised with eerie carvings of mythical beasts, animals that would have roamed the Fertile Crescent at the time, as well as fantastical depictions of humanoid figures. Carved into the pillars, alongside the representations of animals, are symbols that look like *dingirs,* the Sumerian cuneiform that means "star" or "god."

Though only a small portion of the site has been uncovered, it is already clear that its scope and complexity would have been a staggering undertaking for the nomadic hunter-gatherers who then populated the land. Hunter-gatherers who had not yet developed agriculture, let alone advanced tools, and who did not live in towns or cities, still designed and built an artistically advanced and architecturally complex place of worship literally thousands of years before humankind built Stonehenge or the pyramids. Until recently, scholars long believed that only after the development of farming and stable societies could humans have undertaken the building of monuments. So how—and why—did the builders of Gobekli Tepe do it? Could its discovery radically change our understanding of human history? Could our ancestors have been far more advanced than history reveals? And could they have built Gobekli Tepe with the knowledge of—and as a monument to—the beings that were responsible for that advanced technology?

in these walls, which explains how they could have built them so precisely and without any mortar. But the question is, Where would they have learned such a technique?

MYCENAE

One of my favorite archaeological places in the world is in Mycenae, Greece, about two hours from Athens. There we have these magnificent megalithic walls that are virtually identical to the walls in Sacsayhuaman, halfway around the world. Archaeology tells us, *Well, the reason there's a similarity is that that's just how ancient men built stuff back then.* To me, that makes no sense, that all of these different civilizations would choose the hardest way possible to build. It's like, *Hurray! Yes, let's build a wall. Let's use the biggest, heaviest stones we can find. Let's make it the hardest way possible, and let's not use little stones.* It makes no sense.

Not only are there incredible megalithic walls at Mycenae, but there

The Treasury of Atreus, also known as the Tomb of Agamemnon, sits on Panagitsa Hill at Mycenae, Greece. The doorway to the tomb was crafted with a corbel arch whose lintel stone weighs 120 tons—the largest known lintel stone in the world.

is also a mysterious structure, a tomb excavated into the side of a hill, called the Treasury of Atreus. When you stand inside and look up, it's as if you are inside a perfectly shaped beehive. The acoustics in there are amazing, too. But what's more exciting is that the stones used to build the treasury are humongous. There is one stone that has been hoisted over the entrance of the treasury, and it weighs an estimated 250 tons. Now, I'm not saying that today we could not execute such a feat. But if we would struggle to do so with our modern technology, is it really logical to suggest that our ancestors did it with pivots, little ropes, and wooden rollers?

Another intriguing aspect about Mycenae, especially about the treasury, is that in between the fittings of the stones, no binding agent was used—no mortar—and all the stones fit together so precisely that you can't slip a dollar bill between them, just like in South America. It is perfect. And when you ask modern-day stonemasons to re-create something like this . . . well, Roger Hopkins, an accomplished stonemason in Palm Springs, once said to me, "You couldn't pay me enough money to re-create something like this."

KAILASA

The Kailasa temple in Ellora, India, is one of the most magnificent megalithic sites in the world. Mainstream archaeologists have determined that over a period of 18 years its builders carved away over 400,000 tons of rock. And by that I mean they actually scooped it out of the bedrock. The entire complex is *in situ*—carved out of the stone. It is an absolutely magnificent feat of engineering, and also logistics. If you subscribe to the idea that 400,000 tons of rock was carved away in 18 years, that feat would require the builders to have worked for 12 hours each day, removing 5 tons of rock every hour. Even if they worked for 24 hours a day, that would still mean 2.5 tons of rock per hour. Again, that's 2.5 tons of rock per hour. Who does that? We can't do that today. Apparently no rubble or leftovers were found of the

400,000 tons of rock that was removed. So where did it go? We know that at many other sites where rocks were removed they were repurposed in different buildings. At Kailasa we don't have that, according to archaeologists. So where did all the rubble go?

Hindu mythology tells us that Kailasa was built with a miracle machine called the Bhaumastra. The Bhaumastra was able to carve and cut into rock without leaving behind any type of residue. The carvings that we see at Kailasa are also a huge component of ancient astronaut theory because they depict Hindu mythology come to life: flying shields, cosmic pillars of fire, and weird beings just hanging out in the sky. So my question is, What does it all mean? Because the answer that all these carvings are nothing but a figment of ancient Hindu imagination doesn't hold for me.

Could it be that some of the stories in Hindu mythology, which speak of wondrous machines that were able to carve and cut things or destroy things just with the push of a button, are true? I think it's quite possible that at some point extraterrestrials gave machines or technology to our ancestors. So the idea is that the Kailasa temple was one of the places where direct physical contact happened with extraterrestrials.

Carved *in situ* from the solid rock of a mountain in Ellora, India, the Kailasa Temple is one of the thirty-four Hindu cave temples and monasteries that are together known as the Ellora Caves. According to Hindu mythology, these architectural feats were built with a powerful machine called the Bhaumastra.

PHILIP COPPENS

LEGENDS OF THE LOST

"Ancient knowledge will give us a future." Author, researcher, and investigative journalist Philip Coppens believed this wholeheartedly and pursued the quest to solve the world's great mysteries with the insight, discipline, and intensity of a great thinker. Coppens's work covered a wide range of topics, from ancient Egypt to the Knights Templar, from the assassination of JFK to the existence of extraterrestrials. In addition to his writing, Coppens and his wife, author Kathleen McGowan, produced the radio show *The Spirit Revolution* and gave guided tours through historical and sacred sites in Europe.

With Coppens's passing in December of 2012, *Ancient Aliens* lost a valued and cherished colleague. Coppens leaves us with a wealth of research and discoveries—and the hope that ancient knowledge will provide insights into life, its value, and especially its magical qualities.

MOHENJO DARO

When historians first began identifying the ancient Indus Valley Civilization, two major excavations were of paramount importance: the ancient cities of Mohenjo Daro and Harappa. At both locations there was evidence that the cities' inhabitants had died in a cataclysm. Archaeological evidence revealed people who had died on the spot, in the middle of the street, probably looking up toward something from the sky, which came their way and caused their death.

The question is, What kind of cataclysm killed these ancient people? It's clear it was something instantaneous. Science and archaeology have been unable to determine that it was a natural event like a meteor strike or a volcanic explosion. Without any forensic evidence available, the question becomes, Can mythology shed any light on the answer? The answer is yes. Mythology tells us that Mohenjo Daro and Harappa were both destroyed in a nuclear blast.

When we look at Sanskrit epics of ancient India, like the Mahabharata, we see accounts of wars that deployed weaponry that truly defies belief. Some of the weapons caused widespread destruction and seem to be on a par with our modern atomic bombs. The ancient

Located in what is now Sindh, Pakistan, Mohenjo Daro was once one of the largest and most advanced cities of the ancient Indus Valley Civilizations. Around 1900 BC, the people of Mohenjo Daro mysteriously vanished.

Sanskrit accounts include truly horrific stories not only of people dying, but also of how the blasts were a result of infighting among the gods. Stories that tell of the gods fighting or being displeased with humankind are something we find in so many other accounts and traditions.

These ancient epics are highly detailed and very specific in describing these divine battles. They said that in these wars, the gods unleashed everything they had at their disposal and that nobody stopped them. The fighting grew worse and worse; the destruction grew in scale; and the magical weapons that were used were as powerful as modern nuclear warfare. They described something very similar to what we would call missile attacks. They saw fire being spewed from aerial objects. They saw what they called thunder and lightning, which was the best way they could describe what they were actually seeing in the skies above them. They were trying, in simple terminology, to explain to people who were not there what was happening. And so the question then is, When the ancient Indians refer to fire, is that really what they were seeing, or is that the nearest word they could find to impart what was truly happening?

The ancient Indians were witnesses rather than active participants in these wars. Instead of being fighters, they gave eyewitness testimony of the gods fighting. What was happening was so atrocious, so astonishing, that they were compelled to write it down, and those accounts later became some of the most sacred stories of the ancient Indian tradition.

Now, when we see people lying in the streets holding hands, as in the case of Mohenjo Daro and Harappa, the question then becomes, Could this have been an atomic explosion? The Mahabharata and the Bhagavad Gita clearly suggest that this might be the case. There is further evidence, not so much for these two places but for places nearby, where extreme amounts of radiation were detected, suggesting a connection between the radiation and the events that happened at the end of Mohenjo Daro's and Harappa's civilization.

Some theorists turn to Hindu mythology to explain what may have wiped out the population of ancient cities like Mohenjo Daro and Harappa. Ancient Sanskrit writings describe a powerful weapon called the Brahmastra, which was made by the Hindu god of creation, Brahma.

There have been reports—so far, unconfirmed—that readings taken at Mohenjo Daro are so high on the radioactive scale that the people who died there likely were exposed to radioactive material. We also have reports from the 1980s—again, unconfirmed—that there was radioactive waste found at one of the sites described in the ancient accounts as a place where the gods allegedly engaged in warfare. And it just so happens that near those sites, high radioactive levels have been encountered, resulting in people who were born in that area having birth defects.

So really, there is quite a bit of evidence to suggest that the legends

An illustration of a battle in a seventeenth-century manuscript of the Mahabharata, a Sanskrit epic of ancient India. Ancient Indian texts like this one contain references to magical weapons that were as powerful as modern nuclear warfare.

of the Mahabharata—which says that there were extraterrestrial beings who fought with radioactive weapons and with otherworldly machines, really left some radioactivity behind, and that the end result is still there to this very day—can be measured with Geiger counters and various other scientific instruments.

EASTER ISLAND

Jacob Roggeveen was a Dutch explorer who set out on an expedition in 1721 to find Terra Australis in the South Pacific, but instead found the remote and mysterious Easter Island and its giant Moai statues. When Roggeveen arrived on Easter Island, he encountered two tribes: one tribe had long red hair, the other short hair. It was said that the two tribes had worked together to build the Moai but that the short-haired people labored under the commands of the long-haired people. Later, there was a revolt, and the short-haired tribe basically massacred the long-haired tribe. Very few of the long-haired people survived.

The disappearance of the long-haired people also meant the loss of evidence as to what really happened in the past on Easter Island and about how the Moai came into being. The side of the story that did survive tells us that the statues of Easter Island were erected for very specific reasons and that they "walked" into place, from the quarry near the volcano where they were cut.

On occasion, it was said, the statues selected their own paths, choosing where they were going to go, instead of letting humans dictate their placement. So what we have here is a very interesting story, because really, it's saying that humankind was doing something artistically very beautiful—we go to Easter Island just to see these statues and are in awe of them—but that really it wasn't a human endeavor. It's saying there was definitely a divine component, that there was something more going on than just people carving statues and erecting them in certain places.

> *The statues of Easter Island "walked" into place; the statues selected their own paths, choosing where they were going to go.*

The question is, When these statues were "walking," was it something achieved through technological means, or was there something else going on? Were the gods directing these statues to position themselves in certain places?

The statues of Easter Island are unique to the island. They are made from volcanic rock, and to some extent, when you look at their placement, they seem to be protecting that volcano. They're guarding this volcano. It's a very powerful force of nature, which has to be feared. At first glance, it looks as if the statues are only giant heads. But in the past few years, excavations have shown that the statues actually have entire bodies buried under the soil. They are *not* just standing heads. They are standing human beings or, perhaps more precisely, standing gods.

We're also discovering that there are inscriptions on the buried parts of the statues. These inscriptions are of interest because we are beginning to understand that these statues are not mute—that as well as "walk," they could "talk," if only we could read Rongorongo, the native language. Hopefully the discovery of these inscriptions is going to project us once again into trying to understand the language of the Rapa Nui (the native people of Easter Island), because with each archaeological discovery, more of these statues are being unearthed and more inscriptions of our ancestors are going to be uncovered. We may finally be able to understand what our ancestors were saying when it came to the meaning of why these statues were created.

> *These statues are not mute— as well as "walk," they could "talk."*

Why did the people of Easter Island erect all these statues? "We don't know" is the short answer, and to some extent, it almost seems as if the Rapa Nui are quite unwilling to share this information. Why did they have to go to such extremes, creating hundreds of these statues and placing them at very specific locations? It's something we really have no answer for. We know that there was a divine component. We know that they did it with statues walking all by themselves. So we know that there was technology involved or something otherworldly going on. But the final missing piece of the puzzle is something we haven't been able to find, and if the natives had it, they weren't willing to share it with us.

We really are at a loss to explain how all of this worked, in large part because when the European missionaries arrived on Easter Island, they weren't interested in recording the legends of the native people. They basically disregarded the locals, quickly converting them to Christianity and destroying all of their writings and texts.

As a result, much information was lost. What we are left with are only fragments of Easter Island's history. And what was happening on Easter Island was clearly not just some isolated event, because there are good clues that what was happening on Easter Island was also happening in other parts of the world. For example, we know that the script of Easter Island, which the natives used, is a mirror image of a script that was used in the Indus Valley, thousands of years earlier. The Indus Valley Civilizations of course included the cities of Mohenjo Daro and Harappa. So a rather interesting question is, How did an "extinct" script that was used thousands of years earlier by people on the other side of the world come to be used on Easter Island? Something clearly is missing.

This missing link can be explained in a number of ways. Science hasn't addressed the issue, and so clearly hasn't come up with an answer. It's possible that the statues of Easter Island are indeed far older than we think they are. That they are, in fact, thousands of years old and that the civilization of the Indus Valley is responsible for these statues. Or that the language that had been in use in the Indus Valley thousands of years earlier went into hibernation and then came out again at the time when the statues of Easter Island were created. If the latter scenario is the case, then clearly, there has to be somebody who transported it from place A, the Indus Valley, to place B, Easter Island. And there was really no human means of doing so at that moment in time. Unless we radically rewrite the history of humankind, the more logical scenario is that the Indus language had been in hibernation and that an otherworldly entity decided the people of Easter Island needed a written language in order to carry out the Moai project, and shared with them a script from another part of the world.

I think *when* Easter Island was inhabited is something of a secondary question. We really need to start looking at the question of *who* inhabited it. And I think that's really the most important answer to find right now, because it will show that Easter Island had links with other civilizations, and probably that there was seafaring happening all over the world. Seafaring means that humans actually created Easter Island. If that isn't the answer or we cannot arrive at that answer, then we really have to look toward the most spectacular conclusion, which is that an extraterrestrial component was involved. And in that case, do we really care when it happened? Because that is surely the best news ever, and whether it happened in AD 300 or in AD 1200 is simply unimportant.

Located at the southeasternmost point of the Polynesian Triangle, Easter Island contains 887 monolithic figures called Moai. The tallest statue, named Paro, stands thirty-three feet high and weighs eighty-two tons.

KATHLEEN McGOWAN

POWERFUL RELICS AND SACRED TALISMANS

Bestselling author Kathleen McGowan has a passion for story-telling, history, and research. Her novels explore the lives of some of history's most famous female figures and the impact these exceptional women have had on human civilization. In addition to her novels, McGowan has published a nonfiction book on the power of prayer and spiritual practice based on her in-depth study of Catharism in France. McGowan also produced and hosted the radio show *The Spirit Revolution* with her late husband, Philip Coppens. Together they created over 150 hours of programming focused on personal and social transformation.

THE POWER OF BONES

The idea of saints' bones and relics having power is one that goes back to the very early days of Christianity. In the book of Kings in the Old Testament, we have a story about the bones of the prophet Elijah, and the power of these bones. In this story, a group of Israelites are burying one of their brethren, and in the process of digging the grave for this man, a group of raiders comes by and the Israelites have to hide quickly. In order to hide, they have to throw the body into another grave. But they throw the body on top of the bones of Elijah. As soon as the body hits these bones, the body actually reanimates. The man comes to life and he jumps up. So it's possible that this story from the book of Kings is where this idea of relics being powerful comes from.

By the medieval era, churches known for housing saints' relics became centers of pilgrimage and attracted large donations. As a result, relics became a kind of marketing tool for medieval churches, which led to a lot of fake relics being out there. Because of this, relics are somewhat ridiculed by modern scholars. But when we look at European legends around saints' bones, we find that among the nobility there was a strong belief that relics really did contain some kind of power.

The belief was that if you had in your possession a relic of one of the saints, you carried some of its magic with you. For example, parts of the body of Lazarus are scattered all over Europe because it was believed that if you had some relic from the body of Lazarus, you yourself would have the ability to be resurrected; the relic would give you some kind of magical

A skull reputed to be that of Mary Magdalene, dipped in gold and encased in a golden headpiece, at the Basilique Sainte-Marie-Madeleine in Saint-Maximin-la-Sainte-Baume, France. Medieval legend held that, after fleeing the Holy Land, Mary Magdalene sailed across the Mediterranean to France, eventually retiring to a cave in the Sainte-Baume mountains. At her death it was said she was buried in Saint Maximin.

ability to overcome death, to overcome mortality. The same thing is true with the bones of Mary Magdalene. Wars were fought over the bones of Mary Magdalene because she is present in the most important resurrection stories. Mary Magdalene is there at the resurrection of her brother, Lazarus. Mary Magdalene is the first witness of Jesus's resurrection, so it was believed that Mary Magdalene's bones might possess the power of resurrection. As a result of an extraordinary devotion to Mary Magdalene, actual *battles* were fought for her bones. The dukes of Burgundy and Provence fought each other to possess the bones of Mary Magdalene.

The bones of the saints who were known to be prophets were the most coveted. Being in the presence of relics of a saint who was known to be a prophet, like John the Baptist, for example, could bring you powers of prophecy. John the Baptist was an itinerant preacher who became famous for baptizing people in the Jordan River. He is found in all of the canonical gospels. Legends of his ministry exist in the Koran and in the historical writings of Josephus. But in Christianity, John the Baptist is specifically important because he is known as "the forerunner" or "the precursor"—the person who is supposed to come before the Messiah. The Old Testament says that prior to the Messiah, a prophet will come and announce the arrival of the Messiah. Those are the shoes that John the Baptist fills.

It was believed that the bones of John the Baptist were brought to Europe during the Crusades. In 2010, a sarcophagus was discovered in the ruins of a church in Bulgaria, in a place known as the Island of John. This is a location that has held an annual celebration for John the Baptist for at least fifteen hundred years. Within the ornate marble sarcophagus were six bones. An inscription on the sarcophagus refers to John the Baptist and his birthday or his feast day. Geneticists tested the bones and determined that they are indeed from the first century and come from a man of Middle Eastern origin. So it is possible that these bones are those of John the Baptist.

THE PINEAL GLAND
AND THE PINECONE

The pineal gland, a tiny gland found in the center of our brain, resembles a pinecone. In fact, the word "pineal" actually comes from the word "pinecone" and as a result, the pinecone became a symbol of the pineal gland. The pineal gland secretes the hormone melatonin, but it has also been thought to be the phylogenic relic of a third eye. Based on this theory, the pinecone became a symbol of enlightenment, of opening up to new understandings and perhaps even communicating with other realms or other dimensions.

What's interesting is that we see across many cultures and many traditions that the pinecone is a symbol used in art, in architecture, and in sacred texts. We see the pinecone sculpted and drawn and painted on any number of pieces of art that are about spiritual enlightenment.

There are many depictions of gods holding pinecones. We see these depictions in Egypt, where the staff of Osiris has pinecones on top of it. We see them in the Mayan culture, where we have statues of gods hold-

Depictions of gods holding pinecones appear across cultures, from the Mayans to the Egyptians and beyond. Pinecones are a common theme in Assyrian artwork—this relief of an Assyrian eagle-headed deity holding a pinecone was excavated from the Palace at Nimrud and dates back to 850 BC.

ing pinecones. But perhaps the most compelling and the most frequent of these depictions come from Assyrian artwork, where we see winged gods holding forth pinecones. In these Assyrian depictions, the gods appear to be shaking them. Now, this could be because the female pinecones generated seeds. And hundreds, even thousands, of seeds could go forth from a pinecone. So these could represent the Assyrian gods seeding our planet with wisdom or information.

Certainly it's understandable how ancient astronaut theorists would come by this idea that these Assyrian gods were holding forth pinecones to remind us that we have a pineal gland, a gland that might help us contact other dimensions.

CYBELE

The Romans spent thirteen years building a temple to the goddess Cybele, the guardian of the gateways. The temple housed an ancient black stone, a meteorite, brought from Turkey to Rome, which was said to contain the actual essence of the goddess. When this meteorite was in the temple, Cybele was actually present. Cybele became incredibly important to the Romans. She is a mother goddess, but she's not simply an Earth goddess. She is the mother of the stars. Cybele is often shown standing in a gateway or with a gateway around her, and that is because she was known to be the guardian of time and space. In order to cross the veil and access other realms, you would have to petition Cybele. The fact that Cybele was known as the guardian of the gateway tells us that, perhaps, the ancients were doing something really interesting and really important with time travel, portals, and stargates. And Cybele is essentially the great goddess of the stargate.

SOLOMON'S RING

King Solomon was the son of the famous King David. He was a Hebrew king who shows up in the Old Testament and is most known for his extraordinary wisdom. There are a number of stories within the Old Testament and outside of the Old Testament about Solomon and how he attained his wisdom. Solomon is without a doubt a historical character. There is just too much evidence. There is too much written in the historical record for Solomon not to be real.

One of the lesser known but more fascinating stories about Solomon is the legend of Solomon's ring. Solomon had a magical signet ring that was made of brass, which some accounts say had the name of God engraved upon it, in addition to Solomon's seal, which was a Star of David. The Star of David—two intersecting triangles—is also an alchemical symbol. In alchemy, the intersecting triangles represent the elements of fire and water or the elements of male and female. So many people believe the ring was infused with a kind of alchemical magic. Another story around the ring is that it contained four precious stones, each of which was given to Solomon by an archangel. Each stone had a different type of power.

The ring contained four precious stones, each of which was given to Solomon by an archangel. Each stone had a different type of power.

But it's what the ring was capable of doing that is truly amazing. It is said that this ring gave Solomon authority over all of the realms of animal, of demon, of angel. Solomon could control all kinds of energies with this ring. One of the legends says that Solomon used the ring to entrap demons, which he then used as slaves to help him build the temple. The demons in this story are a little different from how we think of demons today. In modern times we tend to think of demons as related to the devil, as satanic. But in the time of Solomon, demons were seen as potentially extraterrestrial, as in not of this earth. They were mischievous. Sometimes they were industrious, but they weren't necessarily evil. In the case of Solomon we actually know the names of some of the demons. The most important demon in the Solomon legacy is a demon called Asmodeus. It is said that Solomon imprisoned the demon Asmodeus to protect the treasure in his temple.

What's fascinating about Solomon's ring is here we have this incredibly powerful object with the power to rule the world, and then it just disappears from history. Nobody knows what happened to Solomon's ring. But there are some very interesting theories about what could've happened to it and where it ended up.

In the early part of the twelfth century, nine knights founded an order called the Poor Knights of the Temple of King Solomon. We now know these

A view of the Temple Mount and modern-day Jerusalem, seen from the Mount of Olives. Beginning in AD 1120, the Knights Templar were headquartered at the Temple Mount, beneath which, according to legend, they began digging in search of the lost treasure of Solomon.

knights as the Knights Templar. Ostensibly, the order was founded to protect pilgrims who were coming to Jerusalem. What we have found historically is that the Knights Templar were doing something far more interesting than just protecting pilgrims.

It just disappears from history. Nobody knows what happened to Solomon's ring.

The membership of the Knights Templar quickly expanded well past the original nine until it became an incredibly powerful and wealthy organization. They were headquartered in Jerusalem, at the Temple Mount. Legend has it that they were digging under the mount in hopes of finding the lost treasure of Solomon. It's possible that they were looking for Solomon's ring in particular, this incredible ring that would help them to rule the world.

In 1894, British army engineers discovered evidence that indicated absolutely that the Knights Templar had done excavations under the Temple Mount. They discovered subterranean architecture—Gothic pointed arches—identical to Templar structures in France from the same period. In addition, the British engineers found a number of artifacts that directly connected the Templars to the Temple of Solomon. Based on this evidence, we can definitively say that the Knights Templar were digging beneath the Temple of Solomon.

When both the pope and the king of France decided it was time to eradicate the Knights Templar, a number of charges were brought against them in order to outlaw the order. Among the more curious charges brought against the Knights Templar was that they were communing with demons. The most famous of these demons was a bearded figure named Baphomet, and it was said that when they spoke to Baphomet, Baphomet would speak back to them and give them instructions. This idea that the Templars were somehow interacting with otherworldly characters is something that becomes very important and really endures in Templar mythology.

The legend of the demon Asmodeus as the protector and keeper of the treasure of Solomon's temple becomes very important to the Knights Templar. To this day there is a church known to have been a Templar stronghold, the church at Rennes-le-Château in the southwest of France, with a statue of Asmodeus at the entrance. It is the only consecrated Catholic church where you can walk in the door and be greeted by a demon.

Is it possible, given the fascinating connection between the Knights Templar, their rumored communing with demons, and their work digging under the Temple Mount, that the Knights Templar actually found Solomon's ring?

DROPA STONES

In 1938, a Chinese expedition in the region of Bayan-Kara-Ula discovered a very long cave that had murals painted on its walls. These cave paintings depicted the sun, moon, Earth, and stars, all connected by little dotted lines. As the archaeologists explored the cave further, they discovered tombs aligned in rows. These tombs were filled with very unusual skeletons. The skeletons were quite small and had strangely large and elongated skulls. But the most extraordinary discovery that the expedition made within the cave were 716 stone disks we now refer to as the Dropa stones.

The Dropa stones are about fifteen inches in diameter, with a hole in the center, rather like an old long-playing record. They were elaborately carved with a type of hieroglyph that, when first discovered, no one was able to decipher. It was twenty-four years before a team of archaeologists was able to put together a translation of the Dropa stones. The information that was released from the translations was sensational. One of the stones said that a spacecraft had crashed twelve thousand years ago in that region, and another one of the stones referred to the Dropa people arriving in airplanes twelve thousand years earlier. Yet another stone explained that the Dropa people were peaceful and not warlike.

Two of the Dropa stones were sent to the Soviet Union for analysis, and the Soviet scientists discovered an entirely new aspect of these stones. The stones seem to have been radiated in some way and charged with electrical energy. The scientists found that when they tried to play one as if it were a record, it emitted some kind of sound or vibration.

Although there have been efforts to discredit the Dropa stones and the entire story around the Dropa, there is certainly evidence indicating that there is truth to the stories, especially as relates to the Dropa people themselves. In 1933, there was a report of a culture of dwarflike beings coming into confrontation with the Chinese government, and there was a report of a little woman under four feet tall being escorted away by a Chinese soldier.

One of the stones referred to the Dropa people arriving in airplanes twelve thousand years earlier.

There were even reports that this dwarflike culture was being enslaved at the time. In 1995, the Associated Press reported on something that they called a village of dwarfs within a few hundred miles of the original Dropa site. What we know is that cultures of dwarflike beings have been accounted for in China from at least as early as 1933, and this culture seems to come from nowhere. These dwarflike beings aren't related to any other culture in the region, but they must be descended from something, and it is entirely possible that these beings are the modern descendants of the Dropa. This region where the potential descendants of the Dropa exist is entirely off-limits to visitors. It is a forbidden zone.

Photographs exist of the Dropa stones. There are photographs in the Soviet Union, there are photographs in Germany, and there are photographs in museums in China, but the stones themselves are no longer available. The stones themselves have disappeared. A museum curator in China who was once in possession of two of the stones in the collection claims that he was told to eradicate all evidence of the stones. If he was told to destroy the stones themselves and anything related to the stones, then this is certainly evidence of a cover-up.

JONATHAN YOUNG

THE POWERS OF MYTH

Jonathan Young, Ph.D., is an author, a psychologist, and a storyteller who assisted Joseph Campbell for several years at seminars and became the founding curator of the Joseph Campbell Archives and Library. As a professor, Dr. Young created and chaired the Mythological Studies Department at the Pacifica Graduate Institute in Santa Barbara. Dr. Young developed his interest in the power of stories at an early age. One of six children in a well-traveled family, he learned about the Little Mermaid in Copenhagen, the Pied Piper in Hamelin, the Arabian Nights in Baghdad, and the Buddha in India and Japan.

Dr. Young's main area of expertise is personal mythology; his books and articles focus on using stories for self-understanding.

The study of comparative mythology allows us to see similarities in narratives across cultures, to see common experiences, and to identify patterns important to the human experience. The myth of an epic disaster in ancient history, for example, is shared by many cultures. Many cultures tell of the existence of a great civilization wiped away by a cataclysm, typically a flood. We have accounts in a number of places of great floods that happened in ancient times. These cataclysms are described as "the ax of the gods," who were displeased with humans, usually about either our immorality or rebellion. So they send a flood. And a flood has a kind of purging and cleansing effect. The old is wiped away. The new is made possible.

Perhaps the most well-known flood story is found in the Bible. In the time before the sons of God came down to Earth, there lived the shining ones, who were like angels or fallen angels. They came to Earth, found the women very attractive, and produced children with them. The children were giants, the Nephilim, and it was all right for a while. They were large and impressive, but they were not of good character. They were evil and they taught humans evil ways, and this gradually upset God. So God brought the great deluge and it was a great lesson, a great chastisement. But Noah was a good man. Noah was given a chance to live. God instructed him to build a great craft—an ark, as it was called—with very specific measurements and very specific instructions to put two of everything on it. The ark survived the deluge, and life regenerated.

The story of Gilgamesh, the Sumerian legend, is practically the same story. In the Sumerian story the gods created humans, but Enlil, king of the gods, became annoyed with them. He brought drought and he brought pestilence, but the humans still didn't behave, so he decided to destroy them. But Enki, who was the creator god and more compassionate, advised the humans about the coming flood and warned them to prepare an ark. He warned a human named Atrahasis, specifically, who was told to build an ark to certain dimensions to survive the deluge, just as in the story of Noah.

Plato wrote about the destruction of the great civilization of Atlantis, a culture that developed advanced technology but grew lazy and poor in character, and were punished for it. Atlantis was done in by its own hubris. That is, because of the progress, because of the achievements, because of the genius that was Atlantis, arrogance started sneaking in. They started using their great military power to conquer neighbors, just for the sake of domination. They started to take their magic for

An alabaster statue of Gilgamesh, King of Uruk. The myth of the great flood appears in the Sumerian Epic of Gilgamesh, which dates back to the Third Dynasty of Ur (circa 2100 BC).

Top: A depiction of the Inca creator god Viracocha carved into the Gate of the Sun in Tiahuanaco, Bolivia. Viracocha is shown wearing the sun as a crown, holding thunderbolts in each hand, and crying tears of rain. *Bottom:* From the Hindu myth of Manu to the biblical story of Noah, many cultures share stories of a great flood that threatens to wipe out mankind. According to the Book of Genesis, Noah's ark came to rest at the Mountains of Ararat after the great flood.

granted, and use it without moral reasoning. The god Poseidon, who was involved in the creation of Atlantis, was concerned about the arrogance of the people, so he brought down Atlantis. He caused earthquakes and floods, and it was swallowed into the sea.

In the Mesoamerican tradition, the Inca god Viracocha rose from the waters and created people from stones, but the people were useless; they were brainless giants. The gods were very disappointed and so there was a great flood. Then the gods tried again with small stones and that time it worked out. There's an alternate ending that two people survived the flood in sealed caves and, after the waters receded, came out and repopulated the earth.

In the Hopi traditions, the creator god was kind enough to instruct some people to go to the spider woman, and then they were protected by reeds from the great flood and life was able to regenerate. In the Hopi view of the world, we have to be aware that the floods could come as they have in the past and take away all that we have.

There is a wonderful story in Hindu mythology about the time that Manu was washing his hands in a river. He encountered a strange little fish who was anxious and asked for help to escape from a larger fish. The little fish promised that he would give Manu something in return, something of value. Manu

In Plato's works *Timaeus* and *Critias*, Poseidon, the god of the sea, is described as the ruler of Atlantis. At the story's end, the city of Atlantis disappears into the depths of the sea after it falls out of favor with the gods.

DERINKUYU

Bordered on the north by the Black Sea and on the south by the Taurus Mountains, lies Cappadocia in central Turkey. Here wind and water have sculpted strange shapes out of soft volcanic rock. It was in this landscape of mystery and awe that, in 1963, a simple home renovation in the town of Derinkuyu led to an extraordinary discovery: a vast underground city thousands of years old and more than 280 feet deep.

Experts now believe that an estimated twenty thousand men, women, and children once lived in this structure, which extends thirteen stories deep into the ground. Within its dark hallways there is evidence of religious centers, storerooms, winepresses, and even stables for livestock. The entire structure contains fifteen thousand air shafts that bring air to even the deepest of levels.

But just who built this massive underground city? And what mysterious force drove them to live underground?

According to mainstream archaeologists, Derinkuyu was most likely intended to serve as a temporary shelter from invasion, built around 800 BC. But could the underground city be even older? Ancient astronaut theorists believe it is—perhaps by many thousands of years. The Cappadocia region was part of a Zoroastrian empire—a ruling force that recognized Zoroastrianism as its official religion. The Zoroastrian religion—an ancient faith based on opposing forces of good and evil—is widely believed to have influenced both Hinduism and Judeo-Christianity. Developed sometime before the sixth century BC, its chief god is the creator Ahura Mazda. In the second chapter of the Zoroastrian sacred

text, the Vendidad, Ahura Mazda saves humankind from a worldwide environmental disaster—much like the story of Noah in the Hebrew testament.

According to the sacred texts, Ahura Mazda instructs the great prophet Yima to build a kind of underground refuge similar to Derinkuyu. Yima built a multilevel underground city to protect a select group of people and animals, not from a flood, but from a global ice age. The Vendidad calls this "the evil winters." According to many mainstream climatologists, the last ice age peaked around 18,000 years ago and ended around 10,000 BC. Is it possible that Derinkuyu was built as a refuge from a devastating global winter?

Could the sky god Ahura Mazda have been an advanced being from another world? If so, did he provide the technology needed for his followers to build this complex labyrinth as protection from environmental disaster?

helped him and protected and saved him from the larger fish. Sometime later, that strange little fish told Manu that a great flood was coming, that he should make preparations, and Manu did. He built a boat, and as the waters came, he hitched the boat to the horn of the fish, who saved him by pulling him to a high mountain. They say that fish was a manifestation of Lord Vishnu, the great god of the Hindu tradition. By saving Manu that day, he, by extension, saved the entire human race.

One detail that shows up in many of the deluge stories is some kind of craft that enables survival of the flood. In Noah's case it was an ark, and it was a similar vessel for Manu. The Greek story has Deucalion surviving the flood in a chest. The instruction to create something that will enable survival suggests a kind of rebirth motif.

Beyond shared stories of cataclysm, cultures all across the globe have paintings, murals, and sculptures that seem to depict something like space travel or aero travel, long before any such technology existed. From India to Peru—really, in every great culture—there are carvings of scenes that seem to depict a person on a flying craft, or stories of great flying platforms or huge flying birds that are somehow ridden, which sound more like vehicles than animals.

There's a mural in a marvelous church in Kosovo that shows something like satellites or spacecraft. They look like early Sputnik images. There's a painting in the Palazzo Vecchio in Florence, Italy, which shows the Virgin Mary with a strange object hovering over her shoulder. It looks very much like a flying saucer. There's a fresco in Montalcino, Italy, called *The Glorifica-*

Ancient Hindu texts describe flying palaces called Vimana, which are outfitted with weaponry. The texts list four main types of flying Vimanas: Rukma, Sundara, Tripura, and Sakuna.

RUKMA VIMANA

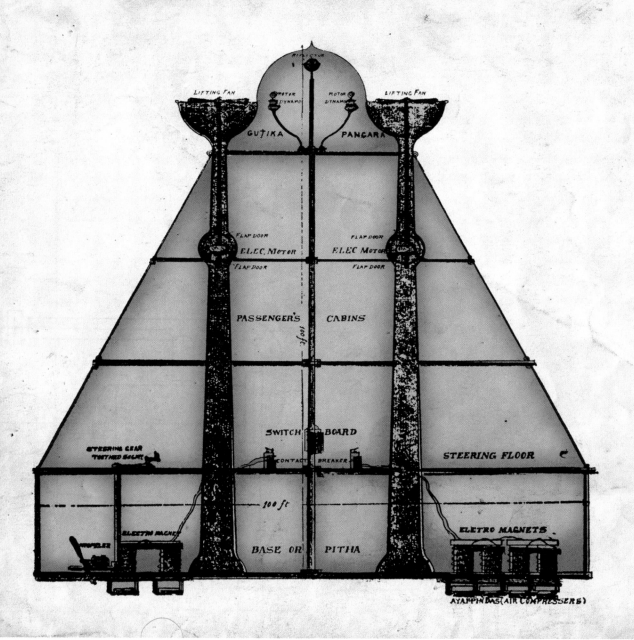

A fresco entitled *Crucifixion of Christ* hangs above the altar of the Visoki Decani Monastery in Decani, Kosovo. In the upper right and left corners of the fresco are flying objects that appear to be spacecrafts.

tion of the Eucharist that shows a stylized image of the Earth with two rods or staffs coming off of it. It looks so much like an early satellite, you would think it had been painted now and that the artist had been inspired by seeing some kind of spacecraft. In Cambridge, England, a painting of the baptism of Christ depicts something saucerlike in the sky, with beams emitting from it, blessing the occasion. In the background of a seventeenth-century fresco of the crucifixion, strange objects fly in the air. Look closely and they appear to be spacecraft.

In the Vedas from India, there are descriptions of flying vehicles called vimanas. They apparently can fly anywhere. There's no obvious means of propulsion, so they can dart about at will. They have armament, something like missiles. And if enemies approach, they can be vaporized. Very high-tech-sounding stuff—and this is from over four thousand years ago. There's one great story where Lord Krishna is piloting one of these amazing crafts, and there's an enemy who manages to make his vehicle invisible. Lord Krishna is clever and quick and is able to follow the sound of the vehicle and still fire off and destroy it. The technology is fascinating, and it sounds very much like space vehicles.

In the Vedas from India, there are flying vehicles called vimanas. They have armament, like missiles.

In the Bible, Ezekiel sees a flying throne chariot, some kind of a vehicle in the sky. It's very clear in the description that the vehicle is being piloted. This vehicle is sometimes described as looking like a great, shining cloud, and when it departs, it departs in a great whirlwind. The use of the word "whirlwind" is interesting because there are other stories that have people going to heaven or back in a whirlwind. I think we should give the ancients some credit. They were intelligent, deep, profound people.

Virtually all of the sacred traditions include interactions between divinities and humans. We have Zeus and the other gods of the pantheon coming down off Mount Olympus to guide us, or cause trouble, or indulge themselves. We have an angel appearing to the Virgin Mary to tell her she'd conceive a new leader. The visitations take several forms. Sometimes a person appears. It's usually in human form that the extraordinary energy presents itself, because it would be too disorienting for the actual human otherwise. So a person appears and gives some kind of guidance or message. Appearances by angels, in Western imagination at least, go back to around the seventh century BC—a ways back.

Hindu philosophy also describes angel-like beings. The devas are creatures that can't be seen, but have great powers. Like angels, they can fly through the sky. Like angels, they have different classes. Some of them interact with humans. The devas are not immortal. They have very long lives but do not live for eternity. They are not omniscient. They know some things but not everything. They aren't the creators of the world. They are divine but they're more like local gods. In fact, when they take physical form, they're very much like humans—a bit larger but still more like us than not. They are intermediaries; that's their importance. An angel is also an intermediary; the word "angel" means "messenger."

In the Koran there is a fascinating category of creatures known as jinn. The English word "genie" is actually derived from the Arabic word "jinn." The jinn are ancient—they were here before humans. They have free will, unlike angels, who must do good. They are capable of good *or* evil. They live in a kind of parallel dimension or world of their own, but they can interact with us. And they are powerful entities you want on your side. They can do powerful and metaphysical things. They can also do dark things. Shaytans, the dark element within the jinn world, are dedicated to evil or trouble. Many of the stories about jinn focus on a mortal striking a deal with or trying to trick a jinn, with serious consequences.

Great turning points in world history have been associated with visitations by supernatural beings.

Great turning points in world history have been associated with visitations by supernatural beings. They will help a leader, a priest, or a hero make some key decision or help him or her at a key moment. They might give these leaders extra powers so that they can accomplish extraordinary things. The Islamic prophet Muhammad, for example, was a man of modest means who lived in Mecca and would take a period of time each year to reflect and pray in a cave in the mountains nearby. During one of these retreats the angel Gabriel came to him and told him his people must look at their gods differently. Gabriel said that Muhammad's people had many icons and divinities but that they were all nonsense; the people were to worship the one god and devote themselves totally to Allah. And the Koran, this extensive book with all its religious insights, was dictated from the angel to Muhammad, who is credited with its authorship.

The emperor Constantine also had a profound encounter with an otherworldly vision. He saw a flaming cross in the sky. He took it as a sign of support from God or the divine realm for his ambitions, and he was indeed successful in his battles. He also decided to end religious intolerance in the entirety of the Roman Empire on the basis of this brief vision.

René Descartes developed the scientific method, which is the foundation for the scientific worldview. The entirety of contemporary civilization is built on it. Who knows what we would not have achieved over the past three hundred years had we not had this system. The source of his inspiration? Descartes said it was a gift from God delivered in a series of dreams.

These stories continue to this day, only in different form: the divine being becomes an E.T. or somebody from another dimension. The details vary but the structure remains the same. We long for connection with something beyond the known. The alien visitors about whom we speculate personify that which is larger than us, that which is beyond our understanding. It's something we dread or something we hope will have potentialities that we do not yet understand. Whatever it is and whatever it means, it is something profound from a world we cannot immediately see, a world more significant, a world of greater and more intense meaning.

RABBI ARIEL BAR TZADOK

GOD'S MAGIC BOX

Ariel Bar Tzadok set out on his religious vocation in 1979 when he left New York to study at Porat Yosef, a leading Sephardic yeshiva in Jerusalem. It was in the holy city where Tzadok studied under leading kabbalists and received his rabbinic ordination (Haredi/Orthodox) in 1983. Upon returning to the United States, Tzadok studied world religions, Jungian psychology, philosophy, and the teachings of many occult systems. Committed to providing practical and realistic biblical teachings, Tzadok established Yeshivat Benei Nviim in 1992 with a focus on the Kabbalah, the biblical prophets, and classical Torah wisdom. A counselor, lecturer, and author, Rabbi Ariel's work covers a wide range of topics including end-time studies, Bible analysis, meditative practices, and human consciousness.

The Ark of the Covenant is first mentioned in the book of Exodus, after Moses descends from Sinai with the Ten Commandments. God commands Moses to instruct the children of Israel to create a chest to house the two tablets on which the Ten Commandments are engraved. But the Ark does not only serve as a receptacle for the Ten Commandments. The Bible tells us that the Ark is also "the throne of God" here on Earth—a physical object through which humans can encounter the presence of God.

From all accounts we believe the Ark of the Covenant was something that was real, an actual physical item with powerful properties that remain mysterious today. We recognize from the biblical stories themselves that the Ark was a weapon. It clearly had a power to it, which was by any stretch of the imagination supernatural.

The book of Exodus recounts that an artisan named Bezalel was in charge of constructing the Ark. It was to be a box within a box within a box with a lid to seal it, roughly three feet by five feet and covered with gold. Crowning the Ark were two cherubim. When God, via Moses, directed Bezalel to create the Ark, he also instructed Bezalel to prepare very specific garments for the high priests who "operated" the Ark, the first of whom was Moses's brother, Aaron.

Aaron was to wear a specific combination of priestly garb. These garments included the famous breastplate of judgment. The breastplate was

inlaid with twelve precious stones, which were to symbolize the twelve tribes of Israel. Embedded in the breastplate was an object called the Urim and Thummim, the function of which is a mystery. No one knows exactly what it was. Aaron also wore a long rope tied to one of his legs, which had bells on the bottom. Why? Because if something ever went wrong when a priest approached the Ark, no one else was allowed to directly retrieve the body, lest they suffer the same fate. Instead, the other priests would be able to pull him out using the rope, if and when he suffered such a fate.

The Ark was concealed within the tabernacle, which only the high priest had access to. And later, when Solomon built the temple in Jerusalem, they kept the Ark in the Holy of Holies, which, again, only the high priest could access. The high priest would enter the Holy of Holies and light a special blend of incense that would fill the entire room. Inhaling the incense would open up synapses in his brain, and he would then telepathically communicate a question to God. In this way, the Ark of the Covenant was a technology for communicating with God.

After the priest telepathically asked his question, a pulsating sound

THE TABERNACLE OF SHILOH

On a parched summer day in July 2013, Israeli archaeologists digging at Tel Shiloh—the historic site of the biblical city of Shiloh—unearthed artifacts that dated back to 1300 BC, a major find that confirmed that, indeed, the city had been occupied and in use in the time of legend. But the most thrilling artifact of human occupation at Shiloh was not the clay pots, stoves, or portions of walls. Instead, a much more mundane find would prove to be the discovery that rocked the archaeological world: man-made holes carved into the solid rock ground. Based on the location and the date of the artifacts, archaeologists believed these holes had held the beams that supported the tabernacle of Shiloh, the ancient sanctuary built to house the most mysterious religious relic in the world, the Ark of the Covenant.

These otherwise innocuous holes were the first physical evidence of the existence of the Ark, the golden chest of incredible, supernatural power, built to hold the tablets of the Ten Commandments. Biblical accounts tell us that ancient people were terrified of the Ark—and that wherever it went, people died. Legends of the Ark's incredible powers—the power to harm, the power to kill, the power to talk to God—have intrigued religious scholars and historians for thousands of years. Could the Ark have been more than legend? And if so, was this mysterious golden chest truly of divine origin . . . or might its powers have come from an even more otherworldly source?

would emanate from the cherubim. These pulsating sounds caused the stones on his breastplate to vibrate and hum. The vibrating stones reflected light and sent out a pattern. Together these created a message in sound and light, which the priest interpreted.

With regard to the Ark being a communication device, it is very clear that the Bible says God showed Moses that the Ark was to be built in accordance with what Moses saw. In other words, the Ark is built as an exact duplicate or reflection of a "heavenly" Ark. We often throw around words like "heavenly" and "spiritual" without pursuing what they actually meant in ancient days. Moses was shown something on Mount Sinai, and he was told, *This is how you build it—follow this example.* And it was meant specifically so that the Ark on Earth would be a communications device that would activate and connect with the Ark in another place, which generically we call heaven.

What did the high priest actually see when he would approach the Ark? It is said that not only did the *presence* of God manifest in those communications, but that the priest also was physically able to see some type of a biocentric pulsating energy field. That's why we understand that the presence of God in the Ark of the Covenant was a life force, a biocentric conscious energy field, which embraced life itself. Indeed, our sages teach us that the entire planet is alive—that the planet is conscious, it is sentient, it has self-awareness, and it is a living entity, as are all the planets.

It was that energy that came through the Ark, which made it alive. Ancient legends tell us that when this biocentric presence of God actually came upon the Ark, the golden cherubim on top were enlivened and they physically moved. The Ark became like God's chariot or God's throne upon the Earth. The only instance that we are aware of where this is repeated in the Bible is in the famous chariot vision of Ezekiel.

I think the Ark is a tool. I think it's always been a tool. Somehow, somewhere there is a reality underlying life that is greater than what our modern science understands. Now, this is where I believe religion and science really must start getting together. From the biblical record it appears that the energy that emanated from the Ark was something electric. The entire Ark, activated by the presence of God, became some type of a biocentric energy field when Aaron, who was the high priest, and his two sons approached it to make an offering. It is said that a strange fire came forth from the Ark and killed them. Ancient tradition describes two beams of literal fire coming forth from the Ark, traveling up their nostrils and burning them from the inside, leaving their entire outsides intact. That sounds to

As the people of Beth Shemesh reap the wheat harvest in the field of Joshua, they look up to see the Ark of the Covenant carried on a utility cart. The Philistines are returning the Ark to Israel.

me like electrocution. So maybe what the Ark projected was something like lightning, and it was some type of an electric field.

I do think we misunderstand the Ark if we believe that it somehow had a mind of its own. The Ark was a technological device. If we accept the fact that the Ark exists, we must understand it as a technological device delivered by some intelligence beyond that which we human beings understand. The Ark was beyond religious or moral parameters. Today, when we get too close to something that is dangerous to us, whether something of a chemical nature or energetic nature, we can die. There is no moral or religious judgment. The Ark was the same. The Ark was of such a nature that its perimeter had to be respected. It was dangerous to touch the Ark. It was dangerous for those not properly prepared to get close to the Ark. There was some kind of energy in the Ark, which had the power to kill. The Levites (the temple workers) were specifically instructed to carry the Ark on very long poles, and they would carry it on their shoulders, but even they were not allowed to touch it. They could touch only the poles. And once the poles were in place in the Ark, that was it—they were never to be removed.

The Ark was a technological device, delivered by some intelligence beyond that which we human beings understand.

It's very clear in the book of Numbers that when the Israelites wandered the desert from Egypt to Canaan, the Ark went forth in front of the camp by three days to prepare their way in the wilderness. The Ark made sure the place where the children of Israel were to go would be safe and would be able to provide for them in the desert. Anybody who's been to the Sinai desert could hardly imagine finding any kind of sustenance there, especially for hundreds of thousands of people. So what the Ark must've accomplished was profound. The sustenance the Israelites relied on was a mysterious substance called manna. The relationship between the Ark and the manna is not explicit in scripture. We know it says that God made manna appear every morning from

The Ark of the Covenant Passes Over the Jordan by James Jacques Joseph Tissot, circa 1896–1902. In this painting, powerful energy emanating from the Ark causes the water of the Jordan River to stop and ascend, allowing safe passage through the Holy Land.

the dew upon the Earth. How did it get there? Because the Ark was meant to prepare the way for and sustain the Israelites, we can make the connection by implication.

Somehow, the power within the Ark had some type of transformational, technological influence over the natural environment. No power on Earth in that day could've ever provided such a thing as manna. If we want to interpret that religiously as a miracle, so be it. But those of us with a more scientific understanding have a different word for that power. It is what we call "extraterrestrial." It is interesting that when Aaron's priesthood was challenged, Moses laid Aaron's staff, which was made of wood, overnight alongside the Ark of the Covenant. In the morning Aaron's staff had blossomed. It had leaves, and it had almonds on it. Now, we might say, *That's a miracle*, but let's try to look at this outside of the myth of miracle and understand it scientifically. What could cause a piece of wood to blossom? Well, if there is some DNA left inside wood, energy can reanimate it. The Ark was the source of this energy. That which we call the presence of God, which dwelt upon the Ark, was a manifestation of this natural life-force energy. And therefore it activated whatever was in Aaron's staff and caused what we would interpret to be a dead piece of wood to blossom and come to life. So again, the Ark not only had the properties of death, but it also had the properties of life.

Legend tells us that when the children of Israel were finally to enter the Holy Land, the priests, not the Levites, were carrying the Ark. According to the legend, they were on the eastern side of the Jordan, and somehow, somewhere, some energy came forth from the Ark, causing the waters to literally stop and ascend. This created dry land for the entire children of Israel to walk on into the Holy Land. And then what? It is said that the priests holding the Ark, instead of passing through the dry land to the other side after the children of Israel, took a step back onto the eastern bank of the Jordan River, allowing the water to then flow. Then somehow the Ark levitated, with the priests holding on, and literally hovered and flew to the other side of the Jordan River.

Once in the Holy Land, needless to say, the reputation of the Israelites preceded them. People were terrified. They had heard rumors of the great and awesome Ark. The book of Joshua tells us that when the Israelites reached Jericho, God commanded them to march around the city walls for seven days, with the Ark in the lead. Somehow, between the stamping of their marching feet, the sounding of the rams' horns, and the power of the Ark, the mighty stone walls of the city of Jericho collapsed and the Israelites enjoyed their first conquest in Canaan.

Several years later, the Israelites took the Ark into battle against the Philistines, but lost and the Ark was captured. The Philistines took the Ark of the Covenant and treated it like any other booty, putting it in the temple of their god. The Bible records that very strange things then started to happen. Death and sickness broke out among the Philistines. In ancient times, they had no understanding of energy or what we would consider similar to radiation poisoning, so they considered this death and sickness to be the result of their god's displeasure. They tried to offer sacrifices in appeasement, but it didn't work. So they said, *Let's get this thing out of here.* And they sent it back to Israel. The same thing happened when it reached the children of Israel. Those people who did not take proper precaution in the presence of the Ark also succumbed to illness and died.

The power within the Ark had some sort of transformational, technological influence over the natural environment.

We must understand that the Torah, the five books of Moses as we have them, were not written to be a comprehensive history in which every detail was included. And therefore there were definite secrets about the Ark—how it was built, why it was built, and what it may have contained. We know only so much about it. We know the Ark had the power to kill. We know the Ark had the power to prepare the way for the children of Israel in the desert. What does that mean? What exactly did it do? That we don't know. But we do know that it had powers and abilities not described in scripture. We know that if and when it was taken to war, it could destroy enemies. It was terribly feared by the enemies of ancient Israel. Its presence was considered so dangerous that people did not approach it, and those who violated its boundaries died.

The book of Zechariah prophesizes that in the days to come, when the

Messiah is to be, that there's going to be a tremendous earthquake in Jerusalem. The Mount of Olives will split, and the split will create a chasm forty-five miles wide. It is said that this earthquake will be caused by some type of sonic vibration created from under the earth, and that the powers from under the earth are then going to arise out of this chasm with the Ark, with what's called the holy ones of God. And this is considered to be A) the return of the Ark and B) the famous coming of the Messiah.

According to the ancient prophecies, when the time comes for divine intervention in human history, the armies of God are supposed to march with the Ark of the Covenant before them.

I think we all know that we're living in very, very unstable times. And I believe the reason the world today is so unstable is that deep within the core of our humanity, we all sense some kind of change is coming. There are so many new things, so many strange things. I believe that somehow, somewhere, we are being prepared for something. And it's only a matter of time before that something is revealed. When that time comes, I believe that, like the ancient legend says, the Ark will be reactivated. Communications will be restored, and we will again have not only that which we have lost, but also that which was meant to be in the beginning. I confess that's an optimistic hope, but it's one that I do embrace.

The Ark of the Covenant represents a very important message to us, that we human beings still have open to us a line of communication with our source, our creator. That creator is who we call God, whom I believe reached out to humanity at Mount Sinai and opened the door to extraterrestrial communication through something like a wormhole, perhaps. Instructions were given at that time how to maintain that contact. And I believe that the secrets of those contacts are still available to those who seek them out.

DAVID WILCOCK

THE WORLD GRID

Author, lecturer, and intuitive consultant, David Wilcock has spent much of his life researching and writing about ancient civilizations, consciousness science, and new paradigms of matter and energy. Inspired by the work of Richard C. Hoagland, Wilcock's extensive research explores the hidden science and lost civilizations behind the 2012 prophecies and the hidden intelligence guiding the universe and the human race. Wilcock theorizes that extraterrestrial forces have been waging a cosmic battle to control Planet Earth—and have been doing so for hundreds of thousands of years.

I f you really want to understand why extraterrestrial visitors built the structures on Earth where they did, you need to understand that all of these structures, almost without exception, are built on a worldwide geometric pattern. This pattern was originally discovered through identification of the primary twelve points that make up the connecting nodes of the grid.

These twelve points, located by Ivan T. Sanderson in the 1960s, are dimensional doorways. They are areas where planes and ships have encountered magnetic anomalies, where compasses start spinning, where dematerialization, in which people disappear and then reappear later on, has happened. At these twelve points, there have been time slips, in which people arrive much too early or much too late at a destination. They are areas where all the crew and passengers of a ship have disappeared into thin air, leaving the

ship behind, eggs still frying on the stove. The Bermuda Triangle, for example, is only one of these spots. Sanderson identified *ten* different points around the world where these kinds of things happen, and when you add the North and South Poles, you get twelve.

What's interesting about these twelve points is that they're equidistant from one another. They exist at 36 degrees north and south latitude. Longitudinally, they're 72 degrees apart from one another above and below the equator. It's when you play connect the dots that you get a geometric pattern called an icosahedron. This is a soccer ball–type shape made out of twenty equilateral triangles. If you flip the icosahedron inside out, you get another geometric shape called a dodecahedron. This is another soccer ball–type shape consisting of twelve pentagons that are all the same size. Between these two geometries, the icosahedron and the dodecahedron, you have a unified grid pattern around the Earth, a pattern that was discovered by three Russian scientists, Nikolai Goncharov, Vyacheslav Morozov, and Valery Makarov. They made this discovery in the early 1970s, working off of the initial twelve points that were discovered by Ivan Sanderson.

What is so mind-blowing is that when the Russian scientists looked at all of the then-identified 3,300 pyramids, stone circles, standing stones,

The Nubian pyramids lie in the Nile Valley, in what is modern-day Sudan. Altogether, there are about 255 pyramids spread out among three separate sites in the region of Nubia, which range in height from twenty to ninety-eight feet. The most elaborate grouping of pyramids is at Meroe, located about sixty-two miles from Sudan's capital city, Khartoum.

temples, cathedrals, and pagodas on Earth, they saw that every single one of them was built on this grid of geometric lines. This includes the Moai stone heads on Easter Island, all the pyramids in Mesoamerica, the pyramids in Giza, the pyramids in Sudan, many of the ancient temples in India, even Angkor Wat in Cambodia—all of them. All over the planet, they were all built on this grid of geometric lines. So the question is, Why would the ancients consistently build only on the grid and not anywhere else?

In 1958, the French mathematician and engineer Aimé Michel published his masterwork, *Flying Saucers and the Straight-Line Mystery.* What is the flying saucer straight-line mystery? If you look in his book, what you find are maps of France in which multiple UFO sightings are charted, and they occur along straight-line paths. One particular diagram shows UFO sightings that took place all on the night of October 2, 1954. There are as many as seven different sightings that all line up in straight lines, and there are groups of parallel lines that form. The same thing happens again when we go to October 7, 1954, and once again we have groups of parallel lines in which there may be as many as three documented UFO sightings—in this case, sometimes four or five—all appearing in a precise straight line.

Another book, *Anti-Gravity and the World Grid,* edited by David Hatcher Childress, contains a fascinating chapter that blows me away now as much as it did when I first stumbled upon it in 1995. It is a chapter by Bruce Cathie on the mathematics of the world grid. I was taken with Cathie's work, because independently of Aimé Michel, Cathie was studying a number of UFO sightings, including some of his own, that took place over New Zealand, and he found the same thing. UFO sightings organize into straight lines. They keep appearing as if they need to be on certain lines and as if their anti-gravity propulsion systems don't even work outside those lines.

What's really strange is that Cathie discovered this on his own and then someone alerted him to Michel's work. It was from reading Michel's work that Cathie discovered that Michel had noticed a pattern in the distances between the UFO sightings. Michel is a darn good mathematician and an engineer, and a very thorough researcher. After extensive research, Michel's conclusion was that the average distance between UFO sightings was 54.43 kilometers.

This got Cathie very excited, because Michel had missed something really important. If you look at the Earth you have, of course, the equator that you can draw as a circle. How many degrees are in a circle? Of course 360. How do we measure units smaller than 1 degree? We chop it up into 60 pieces, and those are called minutes just like how we divide an hour into 60 minutes. You take 1 degree of arc at the equator and you chop it up into 60 pieces, and you get one arc minute. This is also called a nautical

These drawings by Leonardo da Vinci depict an icosahedron (*left*)—a polyhedron with twenty triangular faces—and a dodecahedron (*right*)—a polyhedron with twelve pentagonal faces. In the 1960s, Ivan T. Sanderson located twelve "dimensional doorways" around the world that are all equidistant and that create these shapes when the dots are connected.

mile. What got Cathie so excited was that Michel's magic number of 54.43 kilometers is almost exactly 30 nautical miles. It's a precise harmonic of the spherical shape of the Earth. If you take 360 degrees and then chop up each degree into 60 individual minutes, you have 30 minutes. And the UFOs are always traveling 30 minutes apart.

From this, Cathie was able to derive an incredible reimagining of physics as we know it, including the speed of light and the way that atoms are constructed, and ultimately he was able to create a global grid. Cathie was able to see his grid lines extending over the entire surface of the Earth, and he created a grid that encompasses many different things, such as the Earth's own natural features; many, many different UFO sightings; and the actual trajectories that UFOs in flight would travel along.

They travel along the lines, staying on them, apparently, because the UFOs are powered by the lines in some intrinsic way. To me, this is a fascinating study, and what is even more fascinating is that Cathie's grid has a shape. It resolves into the shape of a perfect cube superimposed inside the sphere of the Earth. Some of the lines also cross in such a way to form an octahedron, and both geometries—the

UFOs travel along the grid lines, because the UFOs are powered by the lines in some intrinsic way.

cube and the octahedron—can, in fact, be enfolded inside each other, forming the simple geometric solid known as the cube octahedron.

At some of the points along this world grid there have been unexplained disappearances. In the case of the Bermuda Triangle, we have more than three thousand documented disappearances in the twentieth century alone, between planes and ships that have simply vanished without a trace. Granted, there have been seemingly credible theories as skeptical explanations for what's going on in the Bermuda Triangle, such as the idea that there are big bubbles coming up through the ocean that swallow up the ships as they're going along. And it is also true that wreckage has been discovered on the floor of the ocean from some of these famous Bermuda Triangle cases. However, in many, many Bermuda Triangle cases, there are planes flying through the air that simply vanish from view. There is no flotsam found on the surface of the ocean. There are no oil slicks. There is no evidence whatsoever of any conventional crash, and no signs of a crash ever turn up, even years later.

The Zone of Silence in Durango, Mexico, is another one of these interesting areas on the Earth's surface that is heavily associated with extraterrestrial activity; strange anomalies in terms of radio, television, and satellite communications; and very curious destructive effects on machinery. The Zone of Silence was first discovered after July 1, 1970, where an Athena rocket carrying two cobalt-57 nuclear warheads malfunctioned in a test flight and crash-landed nose first into a sand dune inside this area. The U.S. government was very concerned, of course, because of the nuclear warhead. So they immediately built a base there to try to find the rocket and identify it. The question is, Why did this rocket malfunction over an area that had already been associated in ancient tradition with strange visitors coming in, with anomalous problems with communication devices? After the initial Athena rocket crashed, a Saturn booster rocket malfunctioned over that area, too.

There have been many strange stories of encounters in the Zone of Silence with extraterrestrial beings who look like us; they may have blond hair, they may have blue eyes, they may be taller, and they may behave a little strangely, but they're friendly and they're helpful to the people. One example is from October 13, 1975, when Ernesto and Josefina Diaz were driving their pickup truck through the Zone of Silence and the rain started to come very quickly. They were worried about a flash flood, and in fact, their pickup did get stuck in the mud. They were very concerned. Then two extremely tall men wearing yellow raincoats and yellow caps showed up and offered to push the truck out of the mud for them. But they didn't want to be seen. The truck was dislodged from the mud almost instantaneously, and when the Diazes went out to look for these two people to thank them, they were gone.

At a small local ranch in the Zone of Silence, the staff were visited by three tall blond people, two men and one woman, who came consistently and were polite almost to a fault. They would ask for their canteens to be filled with water, but they never asked for food—they never asked for anything else. And when the ranchers asked them where they came from, they would only give a vague smile and say, *From above.*

Then you have the case of Ruben Lopez, who was driving through the Zone of Silence when his vehicle's engine began to malfunction. These types of malfunctions are a consistent feature of these vortex areas because they have a scrambling effect on electromagnetic energy fields. So the alternator in your car can start to go out, and this would cause significant problems: it'll make it impossible to drive. This seems to be what happened in this case. Once Lopez's engine went out, he saw five people who appeared to be children, although they were wearing helmets and strange silver one-piece outfits. And when he saw their faces, he determined them to be adult faces. He was quite frightened by this and didn't interact with these people, but nonetheless it's another one of these interesting extraterrestrial contact stories that come out of the Zone of Silence.

The Zone of Silence and other anomalous sites all seem to lie between the 26th and the 28th latitude parallels. The Bermuda Triangle, certain cities in Tibet, Cape Canaveral, and many other sites seem to cluster along these same points.

It seems that the core of what makes the Bermuda Triangle, the Zone of Silence, and similar sites work the way they do is an unacknowledged physics system that's very simple to acquire. All we have to do is fix one Einstein equation. In the conventional Einsteinian view, as you accelerate toward light speed, you gain infinite mass, hence no one could ever travel past light speed because they'd be as massive as the entire universe and it would be impossible to travel. But you can take that equation and, as the Russian scientist Vladimir Ginzburg has done, flip it upside down. Once you do that, you *lose* mass as you approach light speed. You have to answer the question of where the mass is going. But nonetheless, we see this happening on the quantum level all the time. We see particles that seem solid pop over into a wave pattern. So I propose that the key to understanding this science is in realizing that at the quantum level, atoms and molecules are already almost at light speed all the time. That's the quantum flow that's moving through the atom to make the atom exist. And all it takes is a little gentle nudging, such as the spin field within gravity moving at a slightly faster speed, or such as moving the object or vibrating the object with sound, with certain types of light beams, or with energy wave technology to then push those atoms over the light speed boundary. Because once you accelerate the quantum movement in an atom past light speed, you've dematerialized it and brought it into a parallel reality.

So the theoretical foundations are there—we just make one simple change to existing Einstein equations that doesn't violate any laws of physics and now we have a theoretical basis for how dematerialization, teleportation, and even time travel could occur, and more important, why they occur at these certain points on the Earth's surface. If you can build the entire grid off of twelve points that represent doorways between dimensions, then it suggests that the straight lines that make the grid also serve as dimensional portals.

Once you accelerate the quantum movement in an atom past light speed, you've dematerialized it and brought it into a parallel reality.

If we look at the story of the Philadelphia Experiment, it zeros in on one Carlos Allende, also known as Carl Allen. Allende allegedly was part of this group that went through the so-called Philadelphia Experiment in which the USS *Eldridge* dematerialized itself and went through some sort of vortex, and some of the soldiers ended up embedded in the ship's hull as a result of moving into this midway point between dimensions, which, again, is on that same grid line that comes right up along the east coast of the United States, starting down where the Bermuda Triangle is.

There are also grids inside the Earth that are rotating at a different speed, which the Mayan calendar was built to track. One of the cycles in the

Mayan calendar is called a *baktun*, which is 144,000 days long or about 400 years. It was discovered only in 1996 that the Earth's core is rotating with a 400-year rotation period, different from the rest of the Earth. We also know from the Glatzmaier-Roberts model that the Earth's core is geometric in shape. They call it a body-centered cubic iron crystal, because they think it has to be iron down there. But again, the shape is this dodecahedron, which looks like a soccer ball made of twelve pentagons. So you have this rotating geometric core inside the Earth that goes through various phase relationships with the grid on the surface. And when the geometries line up, you get portals that open up. So the Mayan calendar was being used as a tracking system to be able to determine when these portals would open up.

We see that there are in fact lines of energy around the Earth, which appear as a spin field within gravity. We can see that these lines exist through a variety of scientific means, in-

Limestone is a sedimentary rock that has been used to build many ancient sites, including the Valley Temple of Khafre, situated within the complex of the Pyramid of Khafre, the second largest of Giza's pyramids. Some theorists believe limestone was chosen because of its crystalline structure, which can harness energy. *Upper right*: A cluster of quartz. Many natural stones, like granite, are made up of microscopic quartz crystals.

cluding charting out the twelve points around the world where planes and ships disappear. If you connect the lines together, you get the global grid. This is real. It's not a fantasy. That includes Central America and Mesoamerica. Therefore, once you really understand what's going on when someone builds a pyramid, you realize you're looking at a technology that involves the harnessing of this spin field within the Earth's gravity. (I call it the source field because it's the source of all matter, all life, and all consciousness.) We're dealing with the real unified field theory, which is not electromagnetic. The real unified field is going to be found in gravity.

The ancient stone monuments were built to harness that force and that potential to create a funnel-like vortex. The shape of the pyramid literally becomes a funnel so that the energy flowing through it gets put into a spiraling stream. Then the energy has noticeable effects on and benefits for human health, on the health of the Earth, as well as on the ability to create portals for interdimensional travel. This is a high technology. The evidence is all over the world. We're only just starting to recognize what it is and how it functions.

It's especially interesting that stone is the medium that is consistently being used to build these ancient sites. Why are these guys so focused on stone? I believe the key lies in the source field, which is the precursor field that goes into all physical matter in the universe. The source field is what everybody keeps discovering independently. Each person gives it a different name, but it is ultimately the source of all physical matter on a quantum level that flows into the atom itself.

The interesting thing is that when you're building with stone, you're using natural Earth materials that are crystalline in nature. Granite is loaded with small crystals of quartz. Limestone is mostly sand, and sand is mostly silicon. Silicon, of course, is a crystal all of its own. Silicon is the precursor to quartz crystals. So it's this crystalline quality that you see in granite, limestone, and silicon, and what that silicon does with the source field, that determines what we're really dealing with when we look at stone being used as a technology. Stone is a resonator. The crystals within the stone resonate with the source field, the spin in gravity. It's a spin that we don't normally measure, but it is the actual stuff that forms matter and energy. If you didn't have the source field, you couldn't have atoms and you couldn't have molecules. So that's similar to the idea of a candle flame, right? The candle uses wax and oxygen to stay lit, and if you didn't have those two things, *whoosh*, the flame goes out.

Similarly, what causes the electron to keep spinning around the nucleus? Do we ever worry, *Oh my gosh, I hope that the electrons in my atoms are going to stay together, or I might dematerialize?* No. The chair you're sitting in is going to hold you up just fine. You're never going to worry about the atoms running out of juice. They just keep on running and running and running.

But, if you want to run something, you need a power supply. It's basic thermodynamics and conservation of energy. So where the heck is the energy coming from that runs the atoms in your chair? The answer is that there's a source field. It's something that's throughout the entire universe. In fact, it's been calculated that this vacuum energy or zero-point energy is so powerful that if you had one teacup of it, you could instantaneously boil off the world's oceans. That's how powerful this energy is. So think about what would happen if you could just dip a little windmill into that energy field. Well, you could do it by harnessing the power of gravity. The power of gravity, in its essence, is something that's pushing into the Earth. It's a force that pushes into the Earth, and that's what's holding us down, similar to a mosquito that's caught in a screen window as the wind blows through. We're being blown down onto the Earth. That's what gravity really is. So when you understand that, you see that the energy that's causing this blowing-down to happen behaves like a fluid within its own frame of reference. The frame of reference for the fluid is multidimensional. It's not within our three dimensions. We can only measure the effects of the fluid, but we know that it is fluidlike.

Tesla made this discovery. He talks candidly in his journals about the idea that this universal energy behaves like a fluid in many ways. So once we grasp the concept that it's a fluidlike energy, we see that the structure and the shape of any particular object becomes a tool that could lead the object to become a generator. Stone is one of the best generators for the source field because stone is crystalline in nature. That crystal has all these regular geometries, all these facets in it. Those regular geometries capture the vibrating nature of this fluid—this fluid that is gravity—and they make that field become more organized. The shape of a pyramid acts like a funnel for this fluidlike energy, creating a vortex in its center. That's why stone is being used. Its crystalline properties make it excellent to resonate with and create vortex currents within the source field.

Physical matter at the smallest level wants to cluster together into sacred geometry.

If extraterrestrials are landing at Gobekli Tepe or Sacsayhuaman, why? Why would they be landing there? What would they be doing? Again, in my model, I eliminate the ambiguity, because I go in and I look at the data. I look at the data of scientists in Russia, led by Dr. Alexander Golod, who built a 144-foot-tall, steep, obelisklike pyramid. What you find is that these pyramids end up resonating with the source field, with this spin that's in gravity. So it clearly seems that these ancient sites were built to harness this energy.

In our current physics, we do not understand the source field. We do not understand that there is an intrinsic energy that gives rise to physical matter. Physical matter at the smallest level wants to cluster together into sacred geometry. If you take single atoms and shoot them through a nozzle, they do not randomly cluster together. They form what are called microclusters. There is some sort of geometric force that makes those atoms want to cluster together into a geometry rather than other shapes.

This is the same force that shows up as geometric lines around the Earth. Those geometric lines have certain points where they cross over one

Inventor and engineer Nikola Tesla sits in the Colorado Springs experimental station while his Magnifying Transmitter high-voltage generator sends bolts of electricity through the air. The arcs of electricity in the image are twenty-two feet long.

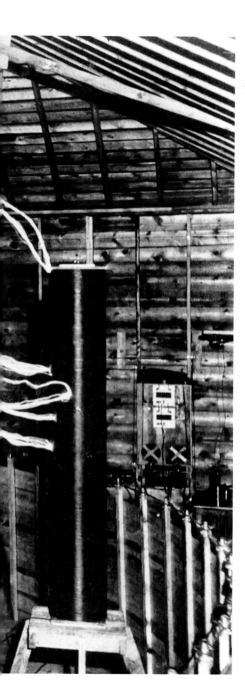

another. The places they intersect are nodes or vortexes. It's all about lines of energy around the Earth that exist from a primordial basis.

There's an interconnection here that suggests that ancient sites were chosen for their energetic benefits, that when you build stone towers and stone monuments at those sites, you get an energetic benefit that you wouldn't get elsewhere. We also see clear evidence of UFO sightings occurring along straight lines. It suggests that the UFOs are using this grid right now. Perhaps gravity shielding needs this geometry in the Earth to function. We haven't been able to measure it so far because we don't know how to measure the source field. We don't know how to measure the seemingly subtle variations in the amount of spin that's in gravity, because gravity just works. We don't worry about it.

But if we could measure the spin fields accurately rather than just by their side effects as we see them now, then I believe this grid would pop right out. I believe the ancients had that technology and that they built these sites where they were because that's where it was easiest to levitate the blocks and be able to get the energetic benefits from them.

But we have to ask ourselves the question, How did the ancients know about this energy grid and how to utilize it? The answer seems to be the fruit of advanced knowledge of physics that we do not yet possess. But to extraterrestrials, perhaps it is well known and widely identified throughout the cosmos.

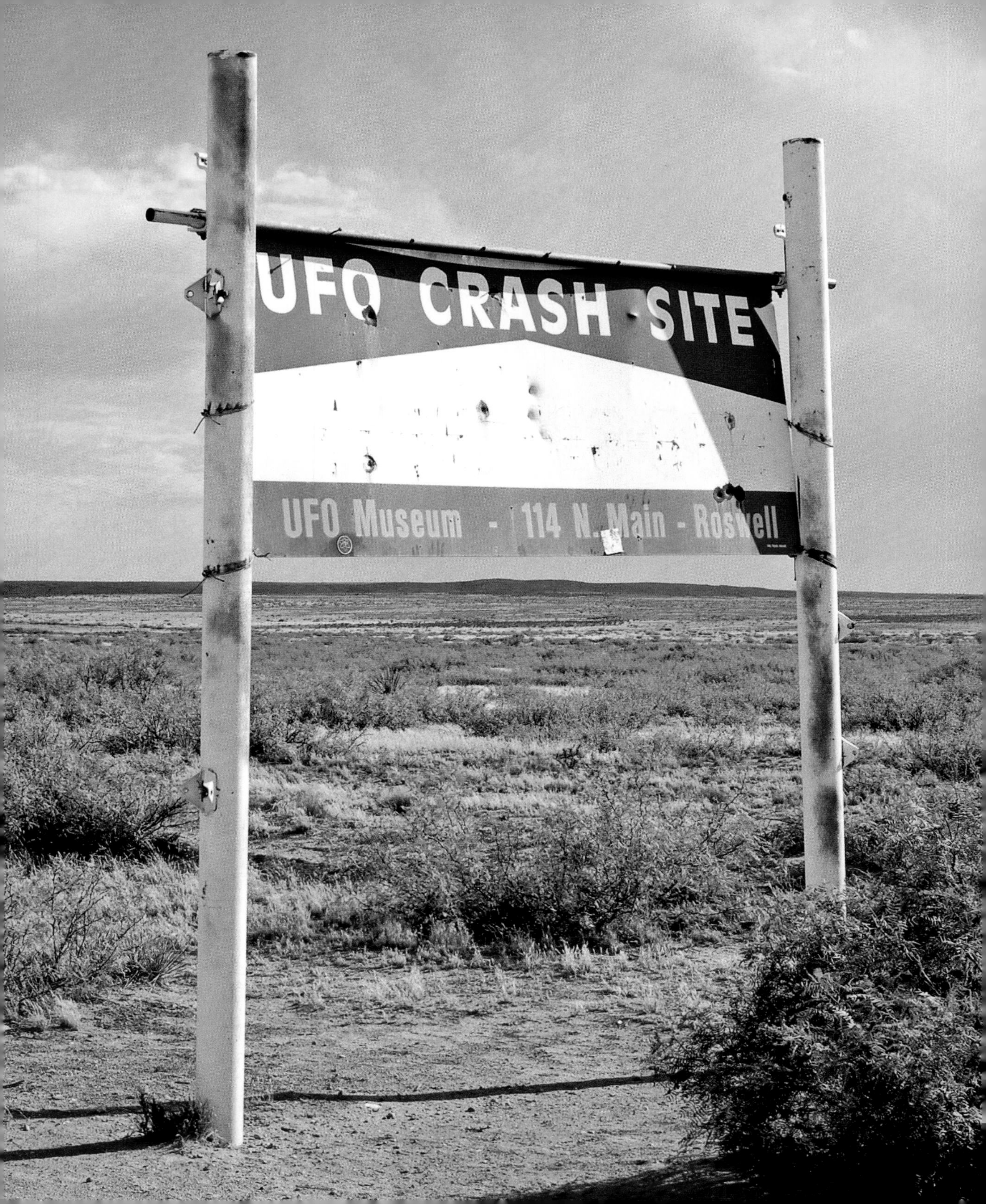
UFO CRASH SITE
UFO Museum - 114 N. Main - Roswell

LINDA MOULTON HOWE

THE ROSWELL FILES

Linda Moulton Howe is a world-renowned researcher and investigative reporter who has devoted her documentary film, television, radio, writing, and reporting career to topics concerning science, medicine, and the environment. An award-winning producer and author, Howe's trusted reputation has often earned her the confidence of insiders, government personnel, and firsthand eyewitnesses of what she calls "high strangeness"——extraordinary cases such as mysterious animal mutilations, UFO sightings, alien abductions, and Earth anomalies.

A resident of New Mexico, Howe has been covering the mystery surrounding the alleged government cover-up of a 1947 UFO crash in Roswell for over twenty years, as the story continues to unfold.

Leased Wire
Associated Press

Roswell Daily Re

47, NUMBER 99. ESTABLISHED 1888   ROSWELL, NEW MEXICO, TUESDAY, JULY 8, 1947

...ovies as Usual

...vies broke and flood waters rolled into the town of ...and Tower, Ill., but while the manager of the movie theater ...eps out the water that has entered the lobby these ...ngsters are standing in line for tickets for the night's per-...mance. (AP Wirephoto).

...me of Soviet Satellites ...ay Attend Paris Meeting

...ris, July 8 (AP)—Indications ...ated today that at least some ...he nations within the Soviet ...would attend the Paris con-...on on the Marshall aid—to...

A Sofia dispatch quoted an ...authoritative source as saying ...presumably Bulgaria will partici-...pate" in the conference, which ...opens in Paris Saturday. The dis-...patch said the Bulgarian consort ...of communists was inclined to reach ...a decision in the matter.

Despite a Moscow radio report ...that Yugoslavia had rejected the ...British-French invitation to par-...ticipate, observers in Belgrade said ...the Yugoslavs still had not replied...

...swellians Have ...tering Opinions ...Flying Saucers

...well is as uncertain about ...flying data, it would appear ...interviews today with a...

Claims Army Is Stacking Courts Martial

Indiana Senator Lays Protest Before Patterson

Washington, July 8 (AP)—Sen-...ator Jenner (R-Ind.) contended ...today that "the high command ...in the European theatre is stack-...ing courts martial against defendants ...in court martial.

In a letter to Secretary of War ...Patterson demanding a full in-...vestigation of army military trial ...procedure, Jenner offered what ...he said was documentary proof ...that:

1. "Prisoners are not being per-...mitted to employ either civilian ...or military counsel of their own ...choice in the preparation and ...presentation of their defense.

2. "Every effort is being made ...to prevent attorneys who were ...connected with the infamous ...Litchfield prison case to practice ...in court martial in the Euro-...pean theatre."

The Indiana senator made pub-...lic a copy of an informal "prob-...ing ship" which he said was sign-...ed by Brig. Gen. Cornelius E. ...Ryan, assistant deputy military ...government headquarters for the ...military government for Germany, ...and written by Col. Francis K. ...Vanderwerker. Jenner told news-...men that the routing slip sub-...stantiated his charges.

The slip, addressed to the chief ...of staff, USFET (presumably US ...forces, European theatre), was ...dated last Oct. 23.

It called attention to the im-...pending arrival of Earl J. Carroll ...and Thomas Lester Petry, Cali-...fornia attorneys, to act as spe-...cial defense counsel for the ...prisoners then awaiting trial by ...general court martial at Frank-...fort Am Main.

Jenner identified Carroll as ...counsel in the court martial of ...Col. James A. Kilian in the Litch-...field (England) prison brutality ...case.

Carroll, then an army captain, ...resigned as assistant prosecutor ...in the Litchfield trials after an ...unsuccessful attempt ...stating also that Carroll ...was being made an by army legal ...officers in the case. Kilian was ...later convicted and fined...

The finding also said that Carroll ...had received widespread publicity ...by violent attacks on the system of...

House Passes Tax Slash by Large Margin

Defeat Amendment By Demos to Remove Many from Rolls

Washington, July 8 (AP)—The ...house passed today the Republi-...can-backed bill to cut income ...taxes by $4,000,000,000 annually ...for 43,000,000 taxpayers, beginning ...Jan. 1.

It goes to the senate where ap-...proval also is forecast.

The vote was 302 to 11, or more ...than the two-thirds majority ...needed to override a presidential ...veto.

The action, which may come ...after Special Master (R-Mass.), ...personally appeal to the house to ...pass the bill by such a decisive ...vote—as to persuade the president ...that the people should have this ...delayed justice.

The measure is identical with ...one vetoed by President Truman ...June 16 as "the wrong kind of ...tax reduction at the wrong time" ...except that the effective date is ...changed from July 1, 1947 to Jan. ...1, 1948.

Congress leaders expect to have ...the revised bill on Mr. Truman's ...desk before the week ends.

The house passed the bill after ...the Republicans beat back a pro-...posed Democratic substitute that ...would have reduced taxes by $3,-...279,000,000 and removed 4,000,000 ...low-income persons from the tax ...rolls completely.

American League Wins All-Star Game

Chicago, July 8 (AP) — The...

Security Council Paves Way to Talks On Arms Reductions

Lake Success, July 8 (AP)—The ...United Nations security council ...today approved an American blue-...print for arms reduction discus-...sions despite a Russian protest ...that the plan would bring about ...a collapse of arms regulation ...efforts.

The vote was 9 to 0, with Rus-...sia and Poland abstaining.

In view of Russia's firm stand ...against the U. S. plan it had been ...believed the U.S. plan might break the big ...power vote to block it.

Soviet Deputy Foreign Minister ...Andrei A. Gromyko gave his warn-...ing before the United Nations se-...curity council in a new effort to ...revise the Soviet working plan ...which already had been rejected ...by the commission for conventional ...armaments.

His challenge was taken up ...promptly by French delegate Al-...exandre Parodi and U.S. Repre-...sentative Herschel V. Johnson, ...who announced their opposition to ...any substitute for the American ...plan.

Gromyko insisted that no pro-...gram for arms reduction could ...succeed unless the U.S. plan was linked ...directly with an absolute prohibi-...tion of atomic weapons.

He declared that the U. S. plan ...approved by the commission did ...not link the problems of arms re-...duction and the banning of atomic ...weapons and, for this reason, it ...offered no basis for a solution.

Gromyko opened debate on the ...arms question as delegates await-...ed another major declaration from ...him later in the day in reply to ...United States and British demands ...for action to reduce armies in the ...critical Balkan situation.

Delegates agreed they were ap-...proaching perhaps the gravest ...moments in U. N. history.

Gromyko said the U.S.-... ...was not a plan by merely A doc-...ument outlining a series of broad...

RAAF Captures
On Ranch in Ro

No Detail... Flying Dis... Are Revea...

Roswell Hard... Man and Wife ...Report Disk S...

The intelligence off... ...509th Bombardment ...n... ...noon Army Air Field to... ...noon today, that the ...came into possession of a ...saucer.

According to inform... ...leased by the depart... ...authority of Maj. J. ...intelligence officer, ...recovered on a ranch ...ward vicinity, after an un... ...rancher had notified ...Wilcox, here, that he ...the instrument on his... ...Major Marcel and a... ...his department went to... ...and recovered the disk... ...stated.

After the intelligence ...had inspected the ins... ...was flown to "higher ...ters.

The intelligence off... ...that no details of the ...construction of the saucer ...been revealed.

Mr. and Mrs. Dan W... ...patiently very the on... ...in Roswell who have... ...they thought was a fly... ...They were willing... ...Wednesday night at... ...minutes before ten o'... ...a large glowing object ...of the sky from the... ...come in a northwester... ...at a high rate of spee... ...flew...

Wilmot said that it a...

RECORD PHONES
Business Office 2288
News Department
2287

ying Sauce
ell Region

King Carol Weds Mme. Lupescu

orner King Carol of Romania and Mme. Elena Lupes
x aboard the S. S. America bound for Cuba and Mexi
May, 1941. A member of Carol's household in Rio
ro said the ex-king and his companion for 23 years
g. and exile were recently married at their ho
pacabana Palace suite. (AP Wirephoto).

iners and Operators Sign
ghest Wage Pact in Histor

A s an investigative reporter, I am amazed by how many leaked documents from the 1940s have come out into the world, laying out details about what really happened at Roswell. And yet we still seem to be overwhelmed by an old story that it was nothing but a Project Mogul weather balloon. *Go away, there's nothing here. There are no UFOs. There are no E.T.s.*

What appears to be the truth about what really happened, though—that comes through documents. There were three objects on radar that night on July 3, 1947; three objects that merged in the air. We have that information. It was on July 4 that a rancher, Mac Brazel, found all kinds of strange silver debris that, when he picked it up, folded like cloth but looked and felt like metal. He knew he didn't understand what he was walking through. He decided to go into Roswell on that Fourth of July and tell the sheriff, "Something has crashed on my ranch." By July 5 or 6, Roswell Army Air Field had assigned a crew including Jesse Marcel Sr. to go to the Brazel ranch and pick up every single item in the debris field. Within a very short period of time, there was a contradictory message

A VERY STRANGE DEBRIS

In early July 1947, a major thunderstorm rolled across New Mexico between Corona and a sleepy town called Roswell, home to a large army air field. Early the next morning, rancher Mac Brazel went out to check on the damage from the storm and came across an extensive area strewn with a very strange kind of debris. He put some of it in his pickup truck and hauled it to the local sheriff's office. The sheriff called the base. The base sent Major Jesse Marcel Sr. to investigate. Major Marcel and his team gathered up all the debris they could find, and the site effectively fell under the jurisdiction and control of the U.S. Army.

A couple of days later, on July 8, 1947, the local newspaper ran a story that stated that an officer named Colonel William Blanchard had issued an order to the army's public information officer, Lieutenant Walter Haut, to announce that the military had in its possession an alien disk and that it was being transported to Fort Worth, Texas, for examination. The report sent shock waves around the world. But what really caused a sensation was when the very next day, the military changed its story and announced that what they had actually found was just a plain old downed weather balloon.

Why would the U.S. Army, whose officers are trained experts at aircraft identification, have confirmed that an alien aircraft had crashed, only to reverse themselves the next day? For both the public and the media, the switch became a huge red flag. Is it possible that the U.S. military actually did find a downed alien spacecraft during the summer of 1947 in Roswell, New Mexico, and a secret government protocol went into effect that called

for the denial of such an event? Although Colonel Blanchard stuck with the revised story, Lieutenant Haut stood by the contents of his initial report his entire life, as did Jesse Marcel, the first army responder to the site at Roswell.

Following Roswell, the public began demanding answers about who or what was behind the unexplained flying objects seen in the skies. The government finally responded six weeks after the Roswell incident . . . not by answering the question, but with President Harry Truman creating the National Security Act.

put out that it was not a debris field of a UFO, but that the debris might've been from some kind of balloon project.

And now we're in the twenty-first century. It's been over sixty years since something from outer space has allegedly crashed out there. Documents have emerged from the mid-1990s that say it wasn't a disk, but something shaped like a wedge of pie—a triangular planiform, meaning it had flat surfaces with curved edges. We've also learned that there wasn't just one crash site in what is called landing zone one, between Corona and Roswell. There was also another crash zone near the Trinity site in northern White Sands. The Trinity site was where, two years earlier, the government had conducted its first atomic bomb test. That was where they discovered five bodies and a craft that was almost intact. Then we learned there was a third crash site. Landing zone three was thirty miles east of Alamogordo and the Mescalero Indian reservation. Whatever crashed there was described as having folded in on itself like an accordion, due to the impact. It was really crumpled.

Why these three different areas? One of the theories was that of the three objects that merged on the radar, a half hour before midnight on July 3, 1947, two were extraterrestrial craft that collided with a secret Project Mogul balloon. They got away with trying to use the mogul balloon as the cover-up for everything, because it contained a tiny seed of truth.

A document dated July 22, 1947 (the same month as the crashes), compiled by the Interplanetary Phenomenon Unit—a unit of the U.S. military—talks about these three landing zones. The first time I read it, I felt a jolt of electricity. All of the questions about Roswell and crashed disks or crashed wedges suddenly came into focus. I really wanted to get to the bottom of what had happened.

There was a period where I and others were going to Roswell, or into that general area, to do some of our own research. A man who had retired from the army, Sergeant Clifford Stone, lived down in Roswell. I visited him several different times at his home, looking at documents. Cliff opened up

Top: White sand dunes at White Sands National Monument, New Mexico. Some reports note a second crash zone near the Trinity atomic test site in northern White Sands. *Bottom:* This photo, taken on March 12, 1967, in Las Cruces, New Mexico, by a New Mexico State University student who was photographing land formations for geology class, shows an unidentified flying object hovering in the air between two cliff sides. The student said the mysterious object made no noise and disappeared when he looked down to change the plates in his camera.

the possibility that maybe a lot of what we were dealing with, including some of the crashes, had been planned. That perhaps the crashed vehicles had been manned by something like what we would call androids (an android would be a robot with a biological form). That what we were dealing with were programmed beings—programmed for very specific tasks. It was as if a door had opened for me. It gave me a context for something that happened a few years later.

A man with firsthand knowledge of one of the autopsies at Wright Field in Ohio said that at the end of the 1940s, a being from one of the New Mexico crashes had been brought in, most likely from the Roswell area. When they inserted the scalpel into the being, they found that what they were cutting was not flesh. It was inorganic material. The beings they had retrieved from the crash sites in Roswell, Alamogordo, and White Sands were not organic in the way we think of ourselves as being.

Perhaps the crashed vehicles had been manned by androids— programmed beings— programmed for very specific tasks.

Then we found out that on July 16, 1947, General Nathan Twining had sent a report to President Truman and General Eisenhower that reads like a science-fiction novel. The report stated that the air force had found something that had three compartments. They thought the upper compartment was the location of some sort of control command that might have been operated robotically. In the middle there were various kinds of equipment. The bottom third housed the propulsion system: there was a translucent ring about thirty feet in diameter, and it appeared to have some kind of water in it. They guessed this was a heavy-water reactor. General Twining wrote, "Upon examination of the interior of the craft, a compartment exhibiting a possible atomic engine was discovered. At least, this is in the opinion of Dr. Robert Oppenheimer, who developed the atomic bomb two years ago." This would have been an impossible concept in 1947. This is Nathan Twining, two years after we dropped two bombs on Japan, saying to the president of the United States and General Eisenhower that inside of this craft is a nuclear reactor. But it's not being used to blow anything up; it's not being used as a weapon. This is a neutron propulsion device.

Philip J. Corso, a former colonel who worked in the Pentagon for the army's research and development office, stated in his own very important book, *The Day After Roswell,* that he had an assignment to take some of the technologies that were retrieved in the nonhuman craft and get them into American corporations. I sat with Colonel Corso in 1997, the fiftieth anniversary of the Roswell '47 crashes, and went over the day that he got the call from his friend General Arthur Trudeau to come to the Pentagon.

As he described it, he went into an office with several metal file cabinets. General Trudeau told him that there was a hugely secret and sensitive project he wanted Corso to work on. General Trudeau walked over to the file cabinets and said, "I want you to come here." He opened up a metal drawer and inside were numerous strange objects. Colonel Corso said it looked like there was some horse hair; it looked like there were poker chips. General Trudeau picked up one of the objects and said, "This is extraterrestrial technology. I want you to physically carry each one of these to a variety of corporations, because our goal is to get these back-engineered and patented inside of the United States of America, to keep these out of the hands of our enemies. I've made all the phone calls." Colonel Corso then proceeded to take packages of extraterrestrial technology to places like Corning Glass, and one person would receive it knowing that General Trudeau himself had set the stage for what the company was going to do. Eventually, there were patents . . . technology that included fiber optics, that included semiconductors, that included lasers.

One of the most fascinating things Colonel Corso told me was that later, General Trudeau told Colonel Corso, "The president [Dwight D. Eisenhower] thinks that the Central Intelligence Agency is an enemy within the

United States. And our work is to keep everything that we are doing out of their hands." That was a revelation to me—that it was at that point that there began a mistrust of agencies, and our government began to splinter. And as the government began to splinter, covering up the presence of extraterrestrial biological entities, the budgets began to splinter. Black budgets began to be directed toward these particular agencies and groups that were trying to ride herd on the back-engineering of extraterrestrial technology in the United States of America.

Another shocking piece of information emerged from a 1952 document, which served as the first annual report by the Majestic 12—a group of military men, scientists, and businessmen who advised President Harry Truman on what they themselves said were celestial interplanetary beings and technologies. In this top-secret MJ12 report, on page 9, it says, "The panel was concerned over the contamination of several security personnel," that I know came in from Los Alamos. "Upon coming in contact with debris, near the power plant of the craft's security, one technician was overcome, and collapsed, when he attempted the removal of a body." They are talking about a nonhuman body—one of the five that they found, outside of landing zone two, at the Trinity site. "Another medical technician went into a coma, only four hours after placing a body in a rubber body bag. All four of these security men were rushed to Los Alamos for observation. All four later died of seizures and profuse bleeding. All four were wearing protective suits when they came in contact with body fluids from the nonhuman occupants. Autopsies on the four dead security technicians are not conclusive. It is believed that the four may have suffered from some form of toxin, or a highly contagious disease. Tissue samples are currently being kept at Fort Detrick, Maryland." Later in the report, they refer to an alien retrovirus. I am often asked, "How could a democracy with elected officials—how could something this huge, with profound implications, be covered up for at least sixty years, and counting?"

Another section of that first MJ12 report contains what I believe is one

THE ROSWELL ROCK

On a clear September morning in 2004, Robert Ridge was tracking deer just eleven miles from the infamous UFO crash site in Roswell, New Mexico, when an unusual object caught his eye: a small, triangular rock sticking out of the sand, which appeared to have an intricate design embossed on its surface. The design—featuring two smaller circles overlaid on a larger circle, each of the smaller circles incised with what look like symbols for the sun and moon—is so intentional and so finely carved that the rock is clearly not the by-product of natural forces. And yet it was not obviously *man-*made, either: the beveled edges of the design were incredibly precise and clear, even under the high magnification of a microscope—suggesting an advanced laser cutting tool was used to carve it. Deepening the mystery of the rock, studies of the stone revealed that not only was it magnetized, but also it was a type of rock not native to the area. Astonishingly, it would turn out that the design rising from the face of the "Roswell Rock" was an exact match for a 120-foot-long crop circle discovered in a wheat field below the Liddington Castle hill fort in Chiseldon, near Swindon, England, on August 2, 1996—almost a decade earlier and 5,000 miles away. Could the matching designs—one discovered so near to the site of the most impactful UFO sighting of the modern era and one part of an ongoing, unexplained phenomena—be "just" a coincidence? Or could they suggest an intentional pattern, even . . . a code from above?

of the most important paragraphs in *any* of the documents that have been leaked. The headline of the section is "Intelligence Gathering and Analysis." The paragraph reads:

> *Based on what is known of the technology and intelligence of the visitors [this was a strange word that they used] it is fairly certain that there will be either sightings or encounters of a spectacular nature. As to purpose and the modus operandi of these visitors we have met, it is clear that, if these visitors had conquest in mind, it would not be difficult for them, given their ability to penetrate our airspace, at will, and their ability to jam radio, telephone, television, and teletype transmissions, let alone power grids.*

This is saying that what everybody has heard for decades—that we were dealing with an intelligence that could bring down whole power grids—is true. Years ago I was told that the Hollywood version of such an event—*The Day the Earth Stood Still*—was a CIA test of the American public to see how people would react to the idea of a nonhuman, with a robot, who had the ability to stop all power on Earth.

The document continues:

> *One of the most difficult aspects of controlling the perception of government attempts at denial and ignorance, is actual control of the press. Until a clear intent is established, with diplomatic relations [meaning with the nonhumans] firmly in hand it is the recommendation of the President's special panel, with concurrence from Majestic 12, that a policy of strict denial of the events surfacing from Roswell, New Mexico, and any other incident of such caliber, be enforced. An interactive program of controlled releases to the media, in such fashion to discredit any civilian investigation, be instituted in accordance with provisions of the 1947 National Security Act.*

Furthermore, in this document they discuss that the constitutional rights of Americans might have to be set aside in the interest of national security. I have been told that Harry S. Truman signed an executive order enacting all of the above. A lot of people have probably suffered a great deal, whether they were civilians or military or intelligence, because the first order of this land, since Harry S. Truman, has been the following: there will be no disclosure of what they know and study about the presence of nonhumans, which, in their own documents, they refer to as extraterrestrial, biological entities interacting with our planet.

> *We are dealing with ancient alien presences right now in the twenty-first century. We're not alone in the universe.*

In defense of those presidents, military personnel, scientists, and corporate leaders who were part of this systematic suppression of the truth, they would probably say that they were superpatriots. And maybe they were. Maybe we have been protected from a lot. But we are now heading toward the middle of the twenty-first century and it is long past the time when our government and all governments should be saying, *We know we're not alone in this universe.* We know that we have been dealing with nonhuman intelligences interacting with this planet for a very long time—that, in fact, we are dealing with ancient alien presences right now in the twenty-first century. It is way past time that the entire human family be told the truth. We're not alone in the universe.

NICK POPE

OBJECTS IN THE SKY

Having served over twenty years in various departments in the UK Ministry of Defence, Nick Pope has been privy to a wide variety of classified information and has researched a vast amount of unexplained phenomenon for the British government. Perhaps the most intriguing assignment Pope had was with a division called Secretariat, where his duties included investigating UFO sightings as well as alien abductions, crop circles, paranormal activities, and anomalies.

As a journalist and author, Pope has written extensively on alien-related topics. A lecturer and consultant, he has also been actively working for the declassification and release of approximately 55,000 documents archived in the British government's UFO files, many of which he worked on during his tenure at the Ministry of Defence.

I worked for the British government's Ministry of Defence for twenty-one years. Three of those years were spent on the UFO project. During that time, two things really changed my mind about the UFO phenomenon. The first was that I had access to a huge archive of classified material going back decades. It was clear to me from looking through this archive that there were many, many cases where these things, whatever they are, were seen by police officers, pilots, military personnel. They were tracked on radar. We had very convincing photographs and videos that we couldn't explain in conventional terms. There's no such thing as an infallible witness, of course, but when the person describing a UFO sighting to you is a member of the military, and particularly air force, that testimony is given a higher degree of credibility than perhaps testimony from members of the public. That was the first thing. The second thing that changed my mind was a handful of very interesting cases that I looked at personally. There are many, many things that I saw both on the UFO project and in my MOD career more generally, but I will not and cannot divulge them. I take my security oath seriously.

The Roman emperor Constantine's vision of a fiery cross at the famed Battle of the Milvian Bridge is one of the incidents featured in the NASA document "Unidentified Flying Objects in Classical Antiquity." The great Italian painter of the High Renaissance, Raphael, depicted the scene in the fresco *Constantine's Vision of the Cross* (circa 1508–1520) in the Room of Constantine, one of the four Stanze di Raffaello in the Vatican Palace in Rome.

It's been suggested that some of these UFO sightings could be attributable to meteors or shooting stars. I don't believe that. Pilots and air traffic controllers are very good observers and they've seen those things before. They can tell the difference. In my experience, around 80 percent of UFO sightings can be explained in conventional terms, case closed. For another 15 percent or so, the information that we have is just too sketchy to make a firm assessment. But in 5 percent of cases, I think there really is some intriguing evidence that there's something above and beyond the conventional, and it's that 5 percent that interests me.

UFO sightings have certainly been with us for all of human history.

Whether it's cave paintings, medieval art, or ancient texts. There are many, many reports of what nowadays we would term "UFOs." Of course back then they were called all sorts of different terms such as "flying chariots." But basically they were UFOs: unidentified flying objects.

One can draw some fascinating parallels between ancient astronaut theory and the more modern concept of UFOs and alien abductions. I suppose from a cultural point of view, our gods have always dwelt in the sky. And sometimes, if you look across a whole range of religions, those gods come down from the sky and interact with human beings. I think when one draws parallels between the ancient and the modern, sometimes really the only thing that sets them apart is the language. It's the labels we put on them.

There is a document titled "Unidentified Flying Objects in Classical Antiquity" that was put out by NASA, which is quite surprising. The document describes a lot of historical accounts of UFO sightings. Of course, they didn't use the term "UFO" or "flying saucer" back in the times of the Romans and the Greeks, but they spoke about things like sky armies, sky shields, and sky ships. One reads accounts by Pliny, Ovid, Livy, Seneca—some of the great thinkers of the age—and they're talking about something that we're obsessed with in the modern era, but it turns out it's been with us for millennia.

In 1566, a newspaper reported a series of strange events that took place on July 27–28 and August 7 over the city of Basel, in northwestern Switzerland. The article describes a battle in the sky between red and black spheres.

I was particularly struck by the sighting from Judea in AD 65, which described a sky army. The idea of the gods at war with themselves is something that has been with humanity for a long time. Now, is this allegorical or is it real? Were these people documenting something that they actually saw in the sky?

One of the most high-profile UFO sightings in the document is Emperor Constantine's vision of a fiery cross in the sky during battle. A battle after which Constantine cemented his position and became emperor of Rome and arguably ruler of the known world at the time. This was particularly significant, because after the battle during which Constantine saw the UFO, Constantine adopted Christianity and it became the official religion of Rome. So there was this complete about-turn. Before that Christianity had been frowned upon and Christians had been persecuted and killed. When it became the official religion of the Roman Empire it became part of the establishment. Arguably, this was a turning point in human history, and it turns out that a UFO sighting may have been at the heart of it.

Why would NASA put out a document like this? Why would NASA seemingly try to ignite a public debate about a subject that publicly doesn't exist? It's a mystery. I think the answer is that while the corporate position of NASA is a very skeptical one, there are a number of people who worked for the agency (who I have met) who are believers.

The modern UFO phenomenon really began in earnest during the Second World War, which was a conflict unlike any other. This was carnage on a previously unimaginable scale in terms of the barbarism, the horrors of the holocaust, and—critically, I think, in relation to UFOs—the detonation of nuclear weapons. If Earth is being observed by intelligent extraterrestrials, how would they have regarded the Second World War? What would they have thought of a people who systemically annihilated a whole group of other people for being a particular ethnicity? What would they have thought of a species that casually deployed nuclear weapons on populated cities

THE BATTLE OVER NUREMBERG

At dawn on the morning of April 14, 1561, citizens in Nuremberg, Germany, awoke to what was later described in a local news flyer as "a very frightful spectacle." Perhaps disturbed from their slumber by the strange noises coming from overhead, they stumbled out of their houses to discover unidentifiable objects in the sky, engaged in what appeared to be an aerial battle. The entire event was memorialized in a broadsheet (the sixteenth-century equivalent of a newspaper) that still exists today in the Zurich Central Library.

The broadsheet account includes a famous woodcut illustration depicting the incident. The library also displays a woodcut of an almost identical sighting in Basel, Switzerland, in 1566. The woodcut advised people to "repent for their sins" and interpreted the extraordinary events as signs from God. Many of the witnesses used religious imagery to explain the objects they had seen, describing crosses flying in the sky—an image strikingly reminiscent of Emperor Constantine's famous vision of a fiery cross, which inspired him to declare Christianity the official religion of the Roman Empire.

Though we may tend to think of UFO sightings as a distinctly modern phenomenon, incidents like the sighting over Nuremberg are shockingly common—going all the way back to antiquity, from Roman orator and senior senator Marcus Tullius Cicero's account of witnessing a bright spherical object appearing in the sky and then dividing into several

smaller spheres, to Christopher
Columbus's recording of a UFO
sighting in the log books of the
Santa María, to nineteenth-
century Japanese testimonies of
encounters with a strange craft,

which seem to link to one of the
single most documented sightings
of all time—the late-twentieth-
century incidents in Rendlesham
Forest, halfway around the globe in
the United Kingdom.

inhabited by noncombatants? Wouldn't that have given intelligent extra-terrestrials real concern at the direction that humanity was taking?

There have certainly been a lot of UFO incidents during wartime, and a lot of important sightings have taken place close to military bases. Now, some people have said that if we're being visited by extraterrestrials, that is the reason: they're concerned about our military activities. They're concerned at the fact that the human race seems to be perpetually at war with itself.

One of the great mysteries of the Second World War involved the so-called foo fighters (a term used by Allied aircraft pilots to describe UFOs and other mysterious aerial phenomena). While most foo fighter sightings involved balls of light, some involved structured craft. During a bombing raid over Turin in 1942, the crew of an RAF aircraft witnessed a UFO that was a solid structured craft about 200 to 300 feet long, performing speeds of around 500 miles an hour. A particularly staggering account of a foo fighter sighting was from 1943 and involved the sighting of an object that was cylindrical in shape, had what appeared to be portholes down the side, and after being pretty much stationary, shot off at a speed of thousands of miles an hour, as reported by the military air crew who witnessed it. After the war it transpired that German and Japanese pilots had seen these things too and thought they were British or American secret weapons.

One story to have emerged from recently released Ministry of Defence UFO files is an allegation that during the Second World War, Prime Minister Winston Churchill conspired with General, and later President, Dwight D. Eisenhower to suppress information about a spectacular UFO sighting witnessed by an Allied bombing crew on their way back from a mission. It's been alleged that the crew of this aircraft encountered a huge UFO with speeds and maneuvers that were clearly way ahead of anything in the infantry of either the Allied or the Axis nations. Apparently, Churchill was horrified by this and said there would be mass panic.

Air Force Sees 'Flying Saucers' On Radar Near Nation's Capital

By JACK RUTLEDGE

WASHINGTON ⑭ — The Air Force today investigated reports that several "flying saucers" had been spotted by radar virtually in its own backyard on the outskirts of the nation's capital.

Not only were unidentified objects seen on radar—indicating an actual substance instead of mere light—but two airline pilots and a newsman saw eerie lights fitting the general description of flying saucers the same night.

Officials could not immediately agree on whether this was the first time radar has picked up flying saucers. Some said it was. All agreed it was unusual.

The objects also were different from the average reported saucer in that they traveled at a relatively slow speed, as well as later disclosing the customary burst that far outspeeds normal airplanes.

One thing was certain. A thorough investigation is being made by the Air Technical Intelligence Center, Wright - Patterson A i r Force Base, Dayton, O. which has been set up to look into flying saucer reports.

Such reports, officials have said earlier yesterday, are coming in faster than at any time since the initial flood in 1947. The current average is about 100 sightings a month.

The flying saucers over the capital were reported late yesterday, about 36 hours after the incident actually occurred.

This is the story as pieced together from Air Force reports, persons involved, and other sources:

An operator at the Air Traffic Control Center at Washington National Airport, across the Potomac from the capital, spotted eight unidentified images on one of his radars ... the area surveillance scope, with a range of possibly 70 miles.

The images were slow-moving, going probably 100 to 130 miles an hour. And they were flying in the vicinity of nearby Andrews Air Force Base.

The control center, operated by the Civil Aeronautics Administration, notified the Air Force and also asked planes in the air if they could see anything.

That was around midnight.

Capt. S. C. (Casey) Pierman of Detroit, piloting Capital Airlines Flight 807, southbound from National Airport, soon reported seeing seven objects between Washington and Martinsburg, W. Va. He said they changed pace, sometimes moving at tremendous speed, at other times hanging almost motionless.

He was careful in his report, and later in an interview, not to identify the objects as flying saucers. He described them as "like falling stars without tails" but added:

"In my years of flying I've seen a lot of falling or shooting stars ... but these were much faster. ... They couldn't have been aircraft. They were moving too fast for that. They were about the same size as the brighter stars, and were much higher than our 6,000-foot altitude."

Another airliner, Capital - National Airlines Flight 610. also reported seeing a light following it from Herndon, Va. to within four miles of Washington.

Saul Pett, an Associated Press newsman, said he saw a "flying saucer" that same night near his home at River Edge, N. J., outside of New York.

HIGHER COURTS

11TH CIVIL APPEALS

EASTLAND, July 22 — The following proceedings were had in the Court of Civil Appeals, Eleventh Supreme Judicial District:

AFFIRMED:
Blanche Spires Bogart, et vir vs. Pearl Spires, et al. Nolan.
Brooks McKinney, et ux vs. City of Abilene, et al. Taylor.

APPEAL DISMISSED:
Southwestern Bell Telephone Company vs. City of Ranger. Eastland.

MOTIONS SUBMITTED:
C. M. Foreman vs. R. P. Stevenson. Appellant's motion for rehearing. Fisher.
Southwestern Bell Telephone Company vs. City of Ranger, et al. Additional Agreement as to file briefs. Eastland.
Toledo Society for Crippled Children, et al vs. Walter G. Kirkbride, et al. Agreed motion to file briefs. Eastland.
Lamesa Rural High School District, et al vs. Cecil Speck. Agreed motion to file briefs. Dawson.
Pete Wessels, et al vs. Rio Bravo Oil Company, et al. Appellants' motion for rehearing. Taylor.
C. B. Whatley vs. R. H King, et ux. Appellees' motion for rehearing. Scurry.
Jesse H. Reynolds, et ux vs. Ona Mangrum. Appellants' motion for rehearing. Eastland.
Clary & Sons Plumbing & Heating vs. Local Trademarks, Inc. Appellants' motion for rehearing. Taylor.
Rita Barber Davis, et al vs. City of Abilene. Appellants' motion for Rehearing. Taylor.

Southwestern Bell Telephone Company vs. City of Ranger, et al. Appellant's motion to dismiss appeal Eastland.
O. K. Pinson vs. H. R. Odom, et al. Appellant's motion for rehearing. Taylor.

MOTIONS GRANTED:
Toledo Society for Crippled Children, et al vs. Walter G. Kirkbride, et al. Agreed motion to file briefs. Eastland.
Lamesa Rural High School District, et al vs. Cecil Speck. Agreed motion to file briefs. Dawson.
Southwestern Bell Telephone Company vs. City of Ranger, et al. Appellant's motion to dismiss appeal. Eastland.

MOTIONS OVERRULED:
C. M. Foreman vs. R. P. Stevenson. Appellant's motion for rehearing. (Written opinion by Judge Long). Fisher.
Pete Wessels, et al vs. Rio Bravo Oil Company, et al. Appellants' motion for rehearing. Taylor.
C. B. Whatley vs. R. H. King, et ux. Appellees' motion for rehearing. Scurry. Jesse H. Reynolds, et ux vs. Ona Mangrum. Appellants' motion for rehearing. Eastland.
Clary & Sons Plumbing & Heating vs. Local Trademarks, Inc. Appellant's motion for rehearing. Taylor.
Rita Barber Davis, et al vs. City of Abilene. Appellants' motion for rehearing. Taylor.
O. K. Pinson vs. H. R. Odom, et al. Appellant's motion for rehearing. Taylor.

MOTIONS DISMISSED:
Southwestern Bell Telephone Company vs. City of Ranger. Additional Agreement as to Filing Briefs. Eastland.

2 File Workmen's Compensation Suits

Two workmen's compensation cases have been filed in U. S. District Court here.

S. Lang of Aspermont has brought suit against The Travelers Insurance Co. of Massachusetts asking for $10,025 in workmen's compensation and $2,000 to cover debts and obligations which he says he incurred as a result of his injuries.

Lang was employed by Frank Woods Associates, Inc., in Stonewall County when injured on Aug. 11, 1951.

The other suit was brought by G. E. Burns of Scurry Couty. He filed his original suit against the Massachusetts Bonding and Insurance Co. in 132nd District Court in Scurry County. The case has been removed to the U. S. Court here.

The plaintiff was employed by Milhoan Drilling Company in Scurry County when he was allegedly injured on Dec. 29, 1951.

Burns was employed at $82 per week. He is asking compensation of 60 per cent of his salary for a total of 401 weeks.

WALLPAPER
PAINT - GLASS - LINOLEUM
WINDOW SHADES - AWNINGS
"Quality merchandise from the nations leading manufacturers"

Abilene Builders Supply Co

1182 North 3rd St.   Dial 4-8553

A news clipping from the *Ames Daily Tribune* dated August 2, 1952, describes a UFO sighting near Washington, DC. Known as the Washington Flap, this incident took place on consecutive weekends, July 19-20 and July 26-27, and involved sightings of strange lights and the detection of unknown objects on the radar of Washington National Airport (now known as Ronald Reagan Washington National Airport).

There would be hysteria. It would shatter people's worldview. It would undermine people's religious faith.

In 1952, Winston Churchill wrote a memo to the Air Ministry in which he asked, "What is all this stuff about flying saucers? What does it all amount to? What can it mean? Please tell me the truth on this issue." Churchill was told that all UFO sightings could be explained as either misidentifications, hoaxes, or psychological delusions. The reply fails to state what the British and the American government actually knew full well, however; that is, that a number, albeit a small number, of these sightings could not be explained in those terms. Churchill was misled.

In the 1980s, this pattern of UFO activity near military forces continued, and in fact escalated, with the Rendlesham Forest incident, near the twin military bases of Bentwaters and Woodbridge. The Rendlesham Forest incident is Britain's most compelling and interesting UFO sighting. It's a case that draws together everything that makes a UFO case important. There's a multiple-witness event. Those witnesses are trained observers. There's radar evidence. There's physical trace evidence in terms of radiation readings, damage on the ground, and so on.

What makes the Rendlesham incident especially important is the number of military witnesses involved. We probably have direct testimony from several dozen people. In fact, including people who have not yet formally gone on the record, there are probably several hundred people who are either direct witnesses to the UFO or were involved in a more peripheral sense. Bentwaters and Woodbridge were Royal Air Force bases, but leased to and operated by the United States Air Force. Bentwaters and Woodbridge were twin bases. In other words, they were so close geographically that they were under one command. Bentwaters/Woodbridge was home to the 81st Tactical Fighter Wing. These were the A-10 aircraft, the so-called tank busters—a critical part of the whole NATO alliance.

There was incredibly high security at Bentwaters/Woodbridge because of the facility's importance to NATO. Shortly after midnight on December 26, 1980, some of the security police and law enforcement personnel at Woodbridge saw strange lights in the forest close to the base. They speculated about the source of the lights. Some thought a light aircraft had crashed. Others thought there might be a fire in the forest. In either event, it was clear to the military personnel that they were looking at something highly unusual and that they needed to go and investigate to determine what it was, to see if there was a potential threat to the installation.

There would be mass panic. There would be hysteria.

Three personnel, John Burroughs, Jim Penniston, and Ed Cabansag, were dispatched to investigate. They drove their jeep out through the east gate of the Woodbridge facility and headed into the forest down a logging track. Eventually the terrain became too rough for them to proceed in their vehicle, so they stopped, got out, and went forward on foot. All the time they were following this light through the trees, and this was unusual; it was like nothing they'd ever seen before. It was almost as if this thing were toying with them, leading them on somehow through the trees.

Eventually they found a clearing in the forest, and in this clearing there was a small triangular craft, about the size of a car or a small tank. The craft was either hovering very close to the ground or it had landed on three legs—a tripodlike device, they thought. This thing was quite clearly a structured craft. This was not a light in the sky; this was not a vague shape. This was a landed structured craft. Someone had built this thing. Someone was operating it. It was clearly under intelligent control.

On the side of the craft, Jim Penniston witnessed strange symbols, which he likened to Egyptian hieroglyphs. He sketched these symbols in his police notebook. The whole situation was extraordinary. Jim Penniston touched the craft. He said it was slightly warm to the touch and felt almost ceramic.

John Burroughs and Jim Penniston had been dispatched to investigate this; this was a military tasking. They had no kind of agenda here. They were simply doing their jobs. When they made their report, they were simply recording what they had seen, what they had experienced. They had nothing to gain by making this report up or embellishing it. I've met John Burroughs and Jim Penniston. I've spent a fair bit of time with both of them. It's clear to me that they are honest and truthful. They were simply doing their best at the time and reporting what they saw and what they felt. It's also clear to me that John Burroughs and Jim Penniston are still quite shaken up by the experience. They would far rather that it hadn't have happened to them.

On the second night of activity, Colonel Charles Halt was at a social function when an airman came in and said to him, "Sir, it's back." Halt said, "What's back?" He was told that the UFO had returned. Halt threw together a small team of people and went out into the forest, in his words, "to debunk this UFO nonsense." He wanted to put the whole thing to bed. He couldn't debunk it, however, because he then himself encountered the UFO.

He saw lights through the trees, different colored lights: blue, red, white. He also saw lights in the sky. Again, there was a sense as with the first night that they were somehow being led, that the lights were under intelligent control. They moved intelligently. They seemed to intention-ally draw Halt and his team deeper into the forest, with the lights reacting to the fact that Halt and his team were closing in on them. It was like a game of cat and mouse taking place in the forest, with Halt trying to find the source of the lights and the lights being quite elusive.

Are we alone or not in the universe? Are we being visited? These are the biggest and most profound questions we can ask ourselves.

Colonel Halt emerged from the forest into a field. He saw a strange glow and lights over the field, and at one point, a beam of light came down from an aerial object and struck the ground very, very close to where he and his team were. They were absolutely spooked by this. Colonel Halt won-dered if it was meant as some type of communication. Was it a warning? It was clear that whatever it was, it was indeed under intelligent control. It spotted Halt and his team and let them know that they had been spotted.

Later on that night Colonel Halt learned through monitoring the ra-dio frequencies that the UFO had actually been directly over the base firing light beams down at the installation. So not only had Halt encountered a UFO firing down at him and his team, there had been another—or possibly the same—unidentified object interacting with the base itself.

Over a series of days, we have multiple reported encounters that in-volve a landed craft with symbols on the side, radiation levels at the land-ing site that are significantly higher than standard background radiation levels, UFOs firing light beams down at some of the personnel, and UFOs firing beams of light down at the facility itself. All this was witnessed and documented by numerous highly trained military personnel, some of them senior in rank.

I'm not saying that this thing was extraterrestrial. But if it was, one can only speculate what it was doing in the area. I suppose one point is

Rendlesham Forest, in Suffolk, England, where U.S. Air Force personnel witnessed a series of unexplained lights and other strange phenomenon in December 1980. The strange events began on December 26, when a security patrol witnessed lights descend into the forest. Then, on December 28, deputy base commander Lt. Col. Charles Halt encountered similar lights while patrolling the forest.

that this was one of the most critical military establishments in the NATO alliance at a time of huge international tension. So it was certainly an interesting place to be.

Many UFO researchers believe that the government withholds important information regarding extraterrestrial life. In my own government

THE UTSURO-BUNE

In the year 1803, numerous fishermen in Hitachi province on the eastern coast of Japan reported seeing a strange vessel wash up on shore. They described the vessel as circular, hollow, and made of metal and glass, with cryptic symbols inscribed on its hull. From the bizarre craft emerged a beautiful woman— clad in clothing of a style and material unrecognizable to the local villagers who had gathered on the beach. In her hands the mysterious woman clutched a small box, which she would not allow anyone to touch. She could not speak Japanese . . . or any other identifiable language. Various historical illustrations of the Utsuro-Bune story depict the

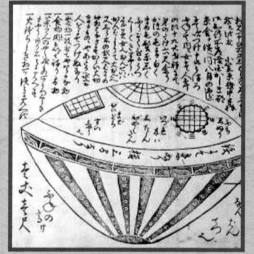

same set of symbols etched in the ship's hull. And fascinatingly, though separated by two hundred years and several oceans, the strange shapes on the craft are eerily similar to those described by Sergeant Jim Penniston in Rendlesham Forest. Could the shared symbology point to an extraterrestrial alphabet? Is it possible the Utsuro-Bune and the Rendlesham Forest craft traveled from the same otherworldly origin? And what does it mean that the Utsuro-Bune washed ashore near the Dragon's Triangle, also called the Devil's Sea, an area of the Pacific Ocean in which more than eight hundred ships have allegedly disappeared?

work on the UFO issue, it was consistently our position to downplay the true extent of our interest and involvement for the British Parliament, for the media, and for the public. Is that a UFO cover-up? Well, it's not exactly a spaceship in a hangar, but it's certainly not telling the entire truth about the phenomenon either.

More and more government and military officials who have been involved with the UFO phenomenon are coming forward and speaking out. Indeed, some governments around the world are opening up their UFO files. There's a kind of quickening of the pace here. It's like we're building up to something, and if there is a great secret to be discovered, I think the disclosure movement is doing its part and keeping interest focused on this fascinating mystery.

My own experience of this is that after I finished my work on the British government's UFO project, I thought it was far too interesting and important just to walk away. So, I stayed involved and I decided to speak out on this issue. Questions of, Are we alone or not in the universe? Are we being visited? These are really the biggest and most profound questions we can ask ourselves. They interest me, and that's why I stay involved with it and why I am so passionate about it.

WILLIAM HENRY

STARGATES

Author and investigative mythologist, William Henry has written extensively on history, archaeology, mythology, and ancient stories of ascension. Based in Nashville, Tennessee, Henry has written eighteen books covering topics from the illuminati, stargates, and sacred mysteries to transhumanism, gnostic texts, and our extraterrestrial past.

Henry's work focuses on understanding spiritual shifts, transcendence, and the expansion of consciousness as we move toward the next level of our human spiritual potential.

———————————————

Throughout the ancient world we're presented with stories of advanced beings who came from the stars. In many instances, these star beings are described as passing through portals or star doors—what we refer to as stargates. The star beings ultimately left their knowledge of these gateways and portals as a gift to humankind. And today we have advanced in our consciousness to the point where we can now understand these stories—understand the advanced knowledge that was gifted to us long ago by these star beings.

Einstein's theory of relativity allowed for something called the Einstein-Rosen bridge, commonly called a wormhole. The concept of the Einstein-Rosen bridge opened up the possibility that we can travel from point A on Earth to point B somewhere else in the universe as if there were nothing in between. The idea of the wormhole revolutionized our thinking. It used to be that we thought we couldn't venture into the stars because the distances were simply too vast. But with the idea of the wormhole came the idea of a cosmic shortcut. A way for humans to become a star-traveling civilization just like the ancient gods.

An artist's rendering of a wormhole, with elements furnished by NASA. The concept and term "wormhole" were actually coined by theoretical physicist John Archibald Wheeler in 1957, more than forty years after Einstein's work on General Relativity.

BIRTHPLACE OF THE STARS

For the ancient Egyptians, the constellation Orion was a celestial embodiment of the gods Isis and Osiris, from whom all of Egyptian civilization and, ultimately, all of human civilization sprang. Orion itself, in their cosmology, contained a nursery of stars that served as the birthplace of all the stars in our galaxy.

Remarkably, millennia later, astronomers made a stunning discovery that affirmed the belief system of these ancient people. On January 11, 2006, the Hubble Space Telescope captured a never-before-seen image of the Orion Nebula, a massive star formation known to be 1,500 light-years from Earth. This panoramic photo revealed something astonishing—more than 3,000 stars in various stages of life. Never before had astronomers been able to witness the different stages of the formation of celestial objects and planetary systems. In fact, they went on to call the Orion Nebula a "star nursery." They believe that thousands of stars and even possibly planets have been created in this mysterious cloud of dust and gas—this is science aligning with ancient legend.

In my research, I've discovered that the ancient Egyptians knew about stargates and wormhole travel. The evidence I discovered is at the Temple of Hathor at Dendera. The ceiling of the temple is an astronomical painting, and it depicts the gods as ascended light beings traveling on their ships of eternity. When you compare the shape of the ship of eternity to a wormhole, they're a perfect match. And that suggests to me that though the ancients didn't use the term "wormhole" for these time-travel portals, instead calling them ships of eternity, they were clearly talking about the same thing.

Like the ancient Egyptians, the Native Americans have a beautiful and wondrous conception of the afterlife. They believe that our soul continues on after death, that it journeys west to the land of the setting sun, where it comes upon a camping ground in which other souls await the exact right moment to make the great and terrifying leap into the Milky Way, which they call the path of the souls.

The ultimate objective of the soul is to make its way through the gate of Orion, which ultimately leads the soul to the center of the Milky Way galaxy. The Native Americans have the whole afterlife mapped out. In life, they go through training, visualizing this journey and learning the various steps along the way, the various guardians that they will encounter, all the various tools that they could use along the way—everything they will encounter in their soul's journey back to the source.

> *The ultimate objective of the soul is to make its way through the gate of Orion.*

In east Tennessee, where I'm from, we learn the Cherokee creation mythology, which says the Cherokee believe they were created by light beings who came from the Pleiades. Those light beings rode a sound wave through a hole in space over east Tennessee and created the Cherokee as guardians of one of twelve vortexes spread around the planet.

Lakota legend tells us that originally the Big Dipper had an eighth

The ceiling at the Temple of Hathor, Dendera Temple Complex, Egypt. Hathor was venerated by the ancient Egyptians as the Goddess of the Sky and known as "The Sovereign of the Stars," who—among her many roles—welcomed the dead to the next life.

star, and this eighth star was in fact a star tunnel or a hole in space that the ascended beings or the supernatural beings could use as a transportation system to come and go from the Earth. And in fact, this stargate, which is what it ultimately was, connected to a vast transportation system that they refer to as the sacred hoop.

The repetition and the detail of these Native American legends of stargates or star tunnels that link Earth with other star systems make you believe that the Native Americans were in fact in direct contact with extraterrestrial beings who actually utilized these stargates and taught the Native Americans how to access them themselves.

According to Incan mythology, the Ayar brothers, who were called "the children of the sun," manifested on Earth at the day of creation through three mysterious windows that suddenly appeared out of nowhere. When you read this story it sounds suspiciously like a stargate story, as though these children of the sun, these advanced solar beings, possessed some kind of stargate technology that enabled them to manifest on the Earth plane. Maybe the Inca story is a recollection of their utilization of this stargate technology.

The Mayans may have possessed this same technology as well. In April 2015, in Teotihuacan, Mexico, Mexican archaeologist Sergio Gómez made an incredible discovery of liquid mercury running in channels beneath the Pyramid of the Feathered Serpent. This liquid mercury had no apparent purpose to the ancient citizens of Teotihuacan. It's toxic. One theory supported by Gómez is that the liquid mercury symbolized the

The Temple of the Feathered Serpent at Teotihuacan, Mexico. In May 2011 researchers from Mexico's National University discovered a tunnel structure beneath the Temple of the Feathered Serpent. A series of mysterious symbols span the length of the tunnel, which archaeologists believe may be connected to imagery of the Mesoamerican underworld.

> *Nibiru is a star, a gate, and a crossing place. The Anunnaki are actually traveling the stars through stargates and wormholes.*

entranceway or perhaps a gateway into another dimensional realm—a stargate. This is fascinating because the feathered serpent is a symbol of human transformation into a celestial being. So it leads to this idea that this temple and the liquid mercury served a purpose ultimately of transforming humans into celestial beings preparing to journey into the stars.

The ancient Sumerians left incredible evidence or clues of the possibility of wormhole travel as well. The Anunnaki are among the most mysterious and powerful beings of myth and sacred tradition. The Sumerians described them as humanoid but nonphysical spirit beings who had the capability of morphing or phasing into human form. According to Zecharia Sitchin, they came to Earth on a special mission to bring wisdom and also to mine certain materials from the Earth plane itself. Sitchin believed that they came from Nibiru. And when we look to the Sumerian dictionaries, which are the source material from the Sumerians themselves, about what Nibiru is, we learn that it's not a planet as is popularly thought. Rather, the Anunnaki said that Nibiru is a star, a gate, and a crossing place, opening up the possibility that the Anunnaki, as these ephemeral or nonphysical spirit beings, are actually traveling the stars through stargates and wormholes.

In fact, this is what we see in their artwork. When we see the Anunnaki coming and going from the stars to the Earth plane, they are very often coming and going through gateways.

When you see the ancient Sumerian gods traveling through the stars, they're traveling aboard these serpent ships that appear to be coiling transportation systems that look very much like how we would describe a wormhole. So it could well be that the ancient Sumerians were also utilizing wormhole technology.

THE SAQQARA BIRD

Twenty miles south of Cairo and the Great Pyramids stands the formidable Step Pyramid of King Djoser, in Egypt's oldest burial ground, Saqqara—known colloquially as "The City of the Dead." Though less ambitious in scale than the pyramids at Giza, the Step Pyramid of Djoser inspires its own magnificent reverence as the oldest of Egypt's ninety-seven pyramids.

It was here, in 1891, among the haunting echoes of time past, that French archaeologists unearthed the tomb of Pa-di-Imen, an official from the third century BC. Among the various funerary items in the tomb was a small, wooden model of what appeared to be a bird, lying beside a papyrus bearing the inscription, "I want to fly."

The artifact was sent to the Egyptian Museum in Cairo, where curators placed it alongside several other bird figurines. The model sat largely unnoticed until 1969, when Egyptologist Dr. Khalil Messiha noticed that there was something very different about the Saqqara bird: though at first glance it appeared to resemble an idealized bird, closer examination revealed a strange oddity in the depiction of its wings.

"It's interesting, because on one hand, clearly, it looks like a bird because it has eyes, and it has a typical nose of a bird. On the other hand, the wings are clearly not bird wings," explains Professor Uwe Apel, an aerospace engineer. His associate Dr. Algund Eenboom explains further: "At the middle of the rump you'll see the wing is a bit thicker. In this region the lift up is the highest. The whole thing becomes thinner to the end of the wings, and those wings are modeled down. And this is a very modern aerodynamic design."

Could the ancient Egyptians have understood—even possessed—the dynamics of flight, two thousand years before humankind invented the airplane? In 2006, aviation and aerodynamics expert Simon Sanderson built a scale model of the Saqqara bird, five times larger than the original, to test that possibility. The results were astonishing. Sanderson's tests demonstrated that the only thing preventing the Saqqara bird from achieving flight was the lack of a rear stabilizing rudder or elevator needed to maintain balance. Further examination of the Saqqara bird revealed that just such a component might have become detached from the rear undercarriage of the figurine. As Dr. Eenboom clarifies, "Tests show the Saqqara bird is a highly developed glider. And this is a design we use today."

Multiple scholars agree that, at the time of its creation, it is likely the Saqqara bird could indeed have flown. If so, how did the ancient Egyptians develop its design? And could its existence point to wider-spread use of flight in the civilization—flight introduced to them by an outside force?

A carving of Ptah (*left*) and the pharaoh Seti (*right*) at the Great Osiris Temple at Abydos, Egypt. As seen here, Ptah was usually represented as a man with green skin, holding a scepter that combined three powerful Egyptian religious symbols: The Ankh (the sign of life), the Djed pillar (symbol of stability), and the Was scepter (symbolizing power).

In the Epic of Gilgamesh, we encounter another very good example of ancient time travel and portal travel. We see Gilgamesh entering a gateway flanked by squiggly lines that symbolize either vibration or water. And it's clear that he has been successful in his quest to find the gate of the gods and is actually traveling through that gate.

One of the great questions that arises when you look at this ancient artwork is, Were those beings actually extraterrestrials that traveled to ancient Sumer, North and South America, and Egypt, using these gateways?

The ancient Egyptians made it clear that they were in contact with extraterrestrial civilizations. They describe beings from the star system Orion and in particular, one god, Ptah, who came from Sirius. Now, Ptah is also the god the ancient Egyptians believed crafted or fashioned the human body. He's also the god of technology. So Ptah came here from Sirius, fashioned the human body, and taught the ancient Egyptians how to resurrect the body, or how to become a celestial or star being so that they could join the other celestial or star beings, the extraterrestrials, and travel the cosmos.

At Saqqara, we find the pyramid texts, some of the oldest religious texts in the world. These texts are devoted to the concept of how to not only preserve the human body but also prepare the soul for journeying into the stars. The pyramid texts are replete with stories of the pharaoh journeying into the stars by ascending a stairway, climbing a ladder, and, above all, flying through the cosmos. What is he flying on? Well, they describe him as flying through the cosmos on a craft called the Ark of the Millions of Years or the Ship of Eternity, which they portrayed on the walls of the temples as looking exactly like a wormhole as modeled in modern science.

We've been waiting for the gate that leads back into the stars to reopen.

One of the amazing things about the Egyptians' journey to the afterlife is that they describe star systems like Sirius not necessarily as final resting places of the soul, but as gateways or stargates along the path of souls to their ultimate destination, the Field of the Blessed. The ancient Egyptians were obsessed with this idea that the afterlife was composed of gateways or

Sirius, the brightest star in the night sky, and the Orion constellation sparkle above a snowy Black Mount in Glen Coe, Scotland. For ages, man has looked to the night sky—to glowing stars and sweeping constellations—and contemplated the possibility that we are not alone in the universe.

passageways that led to higher and finer realms. So you'll find books like the Book of Gates that describe the ability to navigate through twelve different gateways in the afterlife and ultimately join the celestial beings as a star being.

When you go back into the ancient world and look at these stories through the lens of stargate mythology, you recognize that these ancient celestial beings are in fact stargate-traveling time travelers. And that we ourselves could become stargate travelers. This sounds like science fiction, but we're redeveloping this ancient technology now. This is the most exciting moment in human history because we've been waiting for the gate that leads back into the stars to reopen. The same gate as described to us by the Egyptians, Sumerians, Native Americans, Mayans, Inca, and countless other cultures around the world. It's the gate that we all intuitively know exists, and now it's going to become a reality.

motivate us to scour the globe in pursuit of the truth about humanity's past.

We offer a sincere and heartfelt, "thank you."

Ancient Aliens has been—and continues to be—an incredible journey.

Kevin Burns
Executive Producer/Series Creator

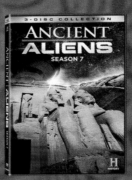